WELLINGTON
Mainstay of Bomber Command

WELLINGTON
Mainstay of Bomber Command

Peter G. Cooksley

Patrick Stephens
Wellingborough, Northamptonshire

10 9 8 7 6 5 4 3 2 1

British Library Cataloguing in Publication Data

Cooksley, Peter G.
  Wellington: mainstay of bomber command.
  1. Wellington (Bomber)—History
  I. Title
  623.74'63'0904   UG1242.B6

ISBN 0-85059-851-6

*Patrick Stephens Limited is part of the
Thorsons Publishing Group*

Printed and bound in Great Britain

Contents

Acknowledgements

It is a truism for authors to state that without assistance their book could never have been written, but never has the cliché been more appropriate than in the case of this work. I give a most hearty vote of thanks, therefore, to the following, who have enthusiastically racked their brains for recollections, found photographs or helped in other ways.

Wing Cdr Dennis F. Ackhurst, RAF; Rear Adm Adrian S. Bolt, CB, DSO, DSC, RN (Retd); Chaz Bowyer; Jeffrey Brown; H.J. Cartwright; R.E. 'Chan' Chandler; Jim H. Colburn; L.W. Collett; William E. Craigen; H.N. 'Joe' Crawshaw; Tom H.C. Claridge; H.E. Dickson; Norman 'Diddy' Didwell; F. Earney; John Ellis; Peter Farnell; J.W. Feltham; Dr. J.A. Frend, PhD; Sq Ldr Raymond Glass, DFC, RAF (Retd); Michael Goodall of the Brooklands Museum; Sqn Ldr A.L. Gwynn, R.A.F. (Retd); Maurice Hare; Reg G. Humphries; H. Kidney; Jerry Monk of *Airmail*; Eric B. Morgan; Norman Nava; D. Jack Paul; W. Priest; Bruce Robertson; Handley D. Rogers; Donald R.W. Saunders, DFC, CEM, RCAF (Retd); Denis Sharp, DFM; The Revd Canon Michael C.G. Sherwood, MA; Ronald Smith; R. Gordon Thackeray, DFM; Wing Cdr Kenneth H. Wallis, CEng, FRAeS, FRSA, RAF (Retd); Geoffrey Wollerton; Harry N.R. Wylie.

Preface

Why a book on the Vickers Wellington? The short answer is that, even though this famous aircraft first flew more than half a century ago, a careful analysis of the aviation books that have been published over the last twenty and more years reveals the unexpected fact that none has dealt with the Wellington from the viewpoint of the crews who flew them, or of personal reactions to a type that was part of their daily lives. The result is that history is currently suffering a severe imbalance in that many people think that wartime Bomber Command operated nothing other than Lancasters; similarly, the unenlightened might be exucsed for believing that there were no other fighters than Hurricanes and Spitfires.

I have written this book in an attempt to correct such mistaken beliefs, remembering that the 'Wimpy' was, in its day, as much a household word as the above-mentioned types. In addition, I always kept in mind the fact that an air force's equipment is only as reliable and strong as the men who operate it, so that this is a record of human achievement, and of the reactions of those who experienced the seemingly indestructible Wellington in many of its varied roles.

Some of those who were interviewed have asked to remain anonymous, so that occasionally names have been changed, while in other instances the stories have survived but not the central characters, and it has proved impossible to discover their names so long after the events.

For some readers the Wellington is no more than a piece of history which enjoyed a strange nickname, and many do not know why the type was so frequently called the 'Wimpy'. In fact, Wimpy was a character in the 'Popeye' newspaper strip cartoon of the period: a strange man, with a consuming passion for hamburgers, who would on occasion announce his full name—'J. Welling-ton Wimpy, Esquire.'

As author, I have met some problems which have been compounded by the lengthy period of service that the aircraft enjoyed. For example, the difficulties of discovering, sorting and checking the earlier recollections may well be imagined. Since the passage of time means that the numbers of those who can recall personal memories of the type in service are steadily diminishing, it is obvious that this is probably the last time that a book preserving the memories of the 'Wimpy men' can be written.

Peter G. Cooksley
London, 1987

Prologue

The great new bomber for the RAF might easily have been known as the Vickers Crecy, in memory of the battle fought by Edward III in 1346. However, one month after the initial production order had been placed in August 1936, the name had been changed to Wellington in honour of the Iron Duke.

Meanwhile, tests had to be continued with the Vickers 9/32, predecessor of the new bomber and, in effect, the prototype Wellington. As part of the normal test procedure, this machine, *K4049*, had been sent to the A&AEE station at Martlesham where, on 19 April 1937, it fell to Flt Lt Maurice Hare, an RAF officer attached to the test establishment, to investigate the dive behaviour of the Type 271.

It was now about 18:00 hours, and all had gone well for both the test pilot and his engineer, LAC George Peter Smirthwaite, who were the only occupants of the machine. Now for the final, and steepest dive of the day. The aircraft responded well to the controls, with the throttle only about half open, and then approaching 2,000 ft, it became clear to a test pilot of Hare's experience that something was wrong. Immediately, he ordered his companion to bale out. Smirthwaite had yet to do so when the dive angle increased until the big machine went over the vertical, flinging the pilot out through the canopy, but leaving him sufficiently conscious to be able to pull the rip cord of his parachute.

The aircraft crashed in a small wood, about a mile south of Martlesham. The fine, calm evening was suddenly rent by the sound of the machine's death throes as it ploughed through the saplings and finally destroyed itself among the more mature trees. In the meantime, Flt Lt Hare landed safely in a ploughed field nearby, only to learn that the unfortunate Aircraftman had not been able to reach the aft exit door in time, and had died in the crash.

Naturally, the total loss of the prototype of a new bomber which had already been accepted for the expanding Royal Air Force was viewed gravely. However, investigation revealed that the crash had been due to a technical fault in the horn balance of the elevator, not to pilot error. The tail control surfaces on the B.9/32 had been designed to provide a larger surface area for aerodynamic balance. These were shielded from the propeller's slipstream at small angles, but became exposed to the full battering of the air when turned through their full angle of travel, so that they failed under the excessive load, and the machine was flung on to its back.

Despite this inauspicious beginning, the Vickers Wellington was to become one of the most famous aircraft of all time, greatly loved by its crews, and for many years the symbol of the might of the Royal Air Force. It served during those last, precious days of peace and then throughout the war that followed, first as a bomber, and then in a variety of roles that ensured its survival even in the heady days after Europe's greatest battle had been won.

Chapter 1
Don't look down!

It is doubtful whether this advice flashed through the mind of Charlie Driver as he sat in the front turret of his Wellington bomber, 15,000 feet above the Heligoland Bight on a cold December day in 1939. But if he did look down, he must have wished that he had refrained: one glance in the direction of his feet would have told him that the floor had been blasted away by the Messerschmitt's latest attack, and that now there was nothing between him and the unfriendly ocean!

The motto of No 9 Squadron was *Per noctem volamus*— 'Through the night we fly'—carried beneath the crest of a bat. But the Weybridge-built Vickers Wellington Ic, *N2983*, with its bold codes *WS-G*, was one of a force made up of Nos 9, 37 and 149 Squadrons of the RAF that was now flying in four tight formations on a *daylight* mission, under bright blue skies. Officialdom believed that bombers required no fighter escort, as their combined crossfire supposedly afforded sufficient protection against enemy interceptors. The theory was fine, but in practice ...

It had all started on the previous day, Sunday 17 December, when 18-year-old Driver had returned from leave to learn that Monday was to be marked by a 'flap' aimed against the Nazi warships at their base north of the mouth of the Elbe. Aircraftman 1st Class Charles Driver had volunteered to act as a front gunner in the raid. This was the accepted practice of the time: all the bombers' defenders were ground crew who had received indifferent training, since the only opportunities they had for perfecting their aim were the off-duty times when they snatched a chance to fly.

On this evening, too, the Flight leaders and commanding officers of all three squadrons had been summoned to Group Headquarters for a briefing. Here it had been agreed that the formations be led by Wing Cdr Kellett in *OJ-D*. A brilliant pilot and a natural leader of men, Kellett had taken command of No 149 Squadron 'just in time', according to some, but had never had the chance to practise formation flying with the other leaders, or to discuss tactics.

However, the importance attached to the question of flying in tight mutually defensive groups was well illustrated by the emphasis that was placed on it in training. Some pilots had amassed a total of 21 hours' formation practice, which was an impressive figure in those days, although eleven hours was nearer the average.

Formation training had been carried on even after the outbreak of war, and, on Monday 30 October, this had brought tragedy to No 9 Squadron when a flight of three Wellington Is took off from RAF Honington to practice the all-important manoeuvres, forming up into the traditional 'vic' as they swept across the flat Suffolk countryside. At their head, in *L4288*, flew Sq Ldr L.S. Lamb, an officer who had led a section against Brunsbüttel on 4 September, when the war was but a day old.

Until 10:15 hours, all had gone according to plan, but at this point it was apparently decided that extra experience was called for in the tactic believed to ensure fighter evasion—the 'rotating vic', regarded by some aircrew as suicidal. Standard procedure was for the leading bomber, No 1, to hold a steady course, while Nos 2 and 3 to starboard and port swapped places. To do this, No 2 would climb a little and move to port, passing over the top of No 1 with about 30 ft to spare. At the same time, No 3 would lose height and pass beneath No 1.

At an altitude of some 800 ft, the three Wellingtons began this manoeuvre while running in towards Honington village. For a few moments, all seemed to be going smoothly, then No 2—F/O J.F. Chandler's *L4363*, began the manoeuvre to port. Losing sight of his leader as he passed over the top of Lamb's aircraft, Chandler reduced height too soon. Suddenly the upper machine's propellers were scything into the top of the other's fuselage. The port one bit deep, so deep in fact that a great gash that it had carved just aft of Lamb's astrodome was sufficiently wide for the whole of the rear fuselage to break off, and it dropped away, spinning down to earth like an autumn leaf. At the same moment, what was left of the leader's bomber reared up into an impossibly tight loop. As the flying hulk flipped on to its back, the wing smashed across the hapless No 2, and the two aircraft, shedding wreckage as they fell, crashed some 50 yd apart into a marshy meadow a short way from Sapiston Water Mill. Chandler's Wellington burst into flames as it struck a tree and Lamb's nosedived into the soft ground. There were no survivors.

Now, six weeks later, the formation theory was to be tested once more; as it had been on all daylight sorties since the war began. On two previous occasions over and round Heligoland, soon to be known as 'The Hornet's Nest', the formation had seemed to prove its value. One instance had been the attack on 3 December, carried out by 24 Wellingtons led once more by Wing Cdr Kellett. He had flown with such panache that it had been difficult for the rest to keep up with him. 'Go a little slower next time', he had been advised by a friend.

The twenty-four crews, including A/C Driver, were roused at 04:40 hrs on 18 December and stood by until, aboard the 24 bombers, the first take-off was made at 09:27. The leading formation, with Kellett at its head, consisted of six machines in two 'vics' from No 149 Squadron. To their left flew a similar pair of Flights from No 9, while on the left were six more Wellingtons, three from No 149, and three from No 9 squadron, including *N2983* (with the tall frame of Charlie Driver crammed uncomfortably behind the front guns) flying No 3 and piloted by 35-year old ex-Halton apprentice, Sgt John R. Ramshaw. Aft of these eighteen flew No 37 Squadron's contribution: six Wellingtons in three groups of two, line abreast—a difficult formation to defend, even though they were flying stepped down in order to give the gunners a clear field of fire (the remainder were stepped up for the same reason). Only one of this final group was ever to see home again.

The first crack in the mutual protection theory appeared when Duguid and Kelly, flying Nos 1 and 2 in Kellett's second 'vic', were forced to turn back with engine trouble only 30 minutes after take-off. The rest of the attackers continued towards the target, carrying the greater part of the 500 semi-armour piercers for delivery on the Nazi warships—if any could be found not too close to land. In those days of the 'phoney war', attacks that might result in the deaths of civilians were dealt with by severe disciplinary action. Meanwhile, it seemed to some that No 9 Squadron's main Flights were too far ahead, and No 37 bringing up the rear was gradually lost. It should be admitted that these two units were somewhat less experienced in formation flying, although they had been drilled in the 'fighter evasion' tactics of the day. No 9 Squadron had even trained through-out the summer to display their formation skills at the XXVth International Aviation Exhibition in Brussels in July.

From their nose turrets, the gunners in the front of the Wellingtons were in a good position to see the first bursts of anti-aircraft fire; 'flaming onions' in the parlance of the day, a term borrowed from the

First World War flyers. At first this was not troublesome and, as there was nothing to excite the attention of the 'armed reconnaissance' (as reporters of the time would have it) over the Heligoland Bight itself, Kellett swung the formation over Wilhelmshaven and commenced the run in at 15,000 ft.

As the ten aircraft that were keeping close formation bore in, the guns redoubled their efforts, the alert gunners below flinging up a hell of steel at the tight-packed Wellingtons. The enemy's aim was accurate for height, but the shells were bursting behind the formation, otherwise they would have been sending wicked needles of shrapnel into the fabric of the hapless Britishers. Even so, the danger was very real, and the rear gunner of the lead aircraft of the starboard box could be heard enjoining his pilot, Sqn Ldr Harris, to hurry up, while, further back in the same formation, Driver could not help wondering how his friend Ldg A/C Lilley was getting on, cooped up as 'arse-end Charlie' of their *WS-G*.

Meanwhile, overhead, like wolves waiting to go in for the kill, enemy fighters could just be made out, lurking in the dazzling blue of the clear sky, and postponing their onslaught until the bombers were clear of the ground barrage. There were some fifty of them, not only the swift Messerschmitt 109 single-seaters, but also twin-engined, two-seat Messerschmitt 110 *Zerstörer* (destroyers). This was, as far as is known, only the second time that these new types had seen action against British aircraft.

Ten miles from the enemy coast, the bomber crews had spotted a Nazi destroyer leaving a long wake as it sped for the sanctuary of the Elbe estuary. Now they would have to seek other prey. Knowing that a rock-steady handling of the Wellington plus immaculate station-keeping afforded not only the best protection but also the greatest aid to the air gunners when the Messerschmitts came, John Ramshaw in *WS-G*, kept his big machine carefully on course. It had seemed up to now that his Wellington had come through the barrage relatively unscathed but, just when he realized that the interceptors would be with them at any moment, he made the chilling discovery that the radio was out of action, probably as a result of a splinter from an anti-aircraft shell. Ldg A/C Conolly, whose charge it was, held out little hope that the instrument could be repaired.

Then suddenly, without warning, the fighters were all among the bombers, with the two-seaters from I/ZG76 scything in, mostly with beam attacks where they ran less risk from the Wellingtons' defences. From the vantage point of his front turret, A/C Driver caught a glimpse of Kellet's No 3, *OJ-B*, going down

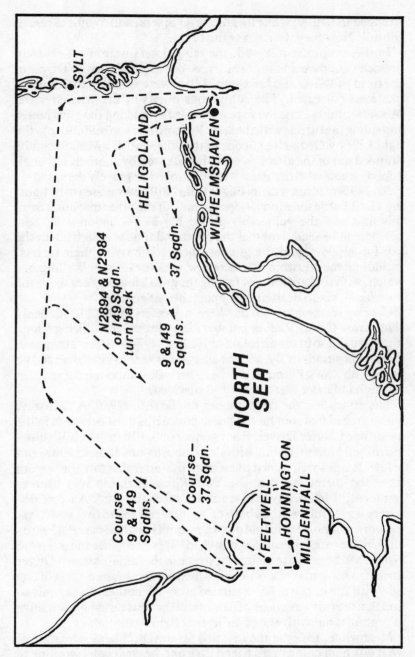

The courses followed by the Wellingtons in 'the Battle of Heligoland Bight'.

wrapped in flames, while its pilot, F/O Spiers, still fought to regain control. Now they were ten against fifty.

In the scrap that followed, the tail gunners were more severely pressed than those in the nose turrets, but even so, Charlie Driver in the front of *WS-G* and 'arse-end' Lilley were spinning their turrets like men possessed. The continuous bursts of fire whenever the Messerschmitts came in range were steadily making the guns hotter and filling the turrets with the stench of cordite. Ten minutes into the fight Lilley yelled, 'I've got one of the buggers!' as a Messerschmitt dropped out of the attack, soon to be followed by another, although nobody knew whether these were destroyed or gravely damaged.

No 149 Squadron with its Flight from No 9 now seemed to be fighting a lone battle for survival, for the bulk of the other machines from this unit and the vulnerably-placed No 37 formation were now nowhere to be seen. Not that the pilots had time to search about the sky for support, and the gunners were too busy in their turrets, including the 'dustbin' retractables underneath the Wellingtons which, with the capability of raising the guns a few degrees above the horizontal, could be used to support the tail gunners.

Coming seemingly from nowhere, a Messerschmitt 110 suddenly shot across the six leading bombers in a vertical turn, firing a long burst as it did so in the direction of Kellett's *OJ-D*. All six gunners in the nose positions let fly, and the enemy was seen to pitch over and go down with a long plume of smoke in his wake, although subsequent research indicates that the Me 110 survived.

The attack left the front gunner of Harris' *N2980*, A/C Doxey, with a grazed foot, but he was not to notice this until later, and in the meantime Charles Driver, front gunner of Sgt Ramshaw's Wellington, found himself dealing with simultaneous attacks from above and below. It was a well-aimed burst from the latter that tore the bottom from the turret, so that the Yorkshireman inside was later to comment, 'I felt pretty cold around my feet and legs'. A worse discovery was to follow when both of his guns refused to fire, and it was the work of a moment to find out why—both had their barrels sheared off. Unable to tell the captain what had happened, since the intercom system had been blasted out of existence in the same moment, Driver turned to leave his useless turret, which was now minus most of one side with the upper perspex carried away in another attack, only to find that the exit was a mass of flames and that there was no alternative to beating it out with one of his leather flying gauntlets.

Meanwhile, Lilley at the rear had his own problems. Unaware of what was happening to his friend up front, he was coolly working to unjam his guns which had been silenced in an earlier attack. The fact that the Wellington was now defenceless was not lost on the Nazi pilots. There was a real danger of the bomber being separated from the others now. However, no one would have guessed the gravity of the situation to judge from pilot Ramshaw's tuneless whistle as he concentrated on keeping formation, oblivious to the Messerschmitts circling above like a pack of wolves, hungry for the kill. Suddenly one broke away from the pack and came in from the rear, taking steady aim at the Wellington that must now surely go down. Realizing his defenceless position, John Ramshaw did the only thing possible and, although hampered by the closeness of the other bombers, took evasive action. The expected end of *N2890* never came, but a shell from the well-aimed hail of fire from the *Zerstörer* ended Walter Lilley's life as he wrestled with his silent weapons.

By now, A/C Driver had gained the cockpit where Ramshaw paused in mid-whistle to mouth 'Are you OK?' For reply, the nose gunner grinned and put up both thumbs. The second pilot, Sgt Hewitt, raised his eyebrows in a silent query and at the same time gestured towards the rear of the machine. Realizing only too well what this meant, the gunner followed the Sergeant aft in silence. They extracted the limp form of Lilley from the turret and laid it on the floor under a covering.

Rising from this task, Driver then made his way to the astrodome. From here the view was one of buckled and twisted engine cowlings and an airframe in places completely shorn of fabric, the torn rags dancing in the air stream. More encouragingly, the engines still seemed to be turning with the familiar rhythmic beat.

While these events were taking place, the other Wellingtons that had come to bomb the naval base were receiving their share of punishment from the defenders. Typical was the case of Harris' *OJ-R* on the right of leader Kellett. Sandy Innes, the Scottish second pilot, was standing in the astrodome, the better to control his gunners. Obedient to Innes' commentary, the occupant of the rear turret, A/C Jimmy Mullineaux, blasted away so enthusiastically that he exhausted all his ammunition of 1,000 rounds per gun. The Flying Officer was therefore forced to crawl aft with short, 300-round belts so that one gun could be kept firing while the other was loaded in the pauses between the fighters' onslaughts. The navigator, Sgt Austin, was able to maintain some support in the ventral position, while at the opposite end of the bomber in the forward turret, A/C Doxey—unlike Driver in *N2983*—had little to do but to keep his mind off the increasing pain in his wounded foot.

Meanwhile, the main No 9 formation on the opposite side of the formation leader, were a long way off and fighting a separate battle that their dangerous position had created. The danger was not entirely their own fault, for the complete formation had had to execute a wide turn to starboard over Wilhelmshaven and back towards the sea. This placed the No 9 formation in an exposed position on the outside of the circle, and the defensive fighters were not slow to take advantage. In addition, the outside flyers found it increasingly difficult to maintain contact with the aircraft on the inside of the circle.

This was particularly the case with Sgt F.C. Petts who was employing full boost and maximum airscrew revs in a desperate attempt to keep his position as No 3 to Sqn Ldr Guthrie's No 1. Petts' navigator, P/O Heathcote, suggested that they drop back and attach themselves to the formation to the rear made up of the six machines of No 37 Squadron, but this idea was rejected, and Petts flew on, making what speed he could.

In the event, his decision was a fortunate one for the rear formation was to be torn to shreds by the fighters. Five Wellingtons were to fall to their guns, leaving only a single survivor; and the latter escaped more by luck than judgement.

The No 37 Squadron aircraft in question was on the starboard side of the leading pair with F/O 'Cheese' Lemon at the controls. Once over the target, in mistake for the bomb door switch, Lemon pressed the one for lowering the flaps. The results were immediate and dramatic, felt as much by the rear gunner, Kydd, as anyone. In a few seconds, it seemed, the Wellington took a tremendous leap into the air before losing height at great speed until it was almost at sea level. At this point the pilot managed to regain control and to weave his way back to base. Meanwhile, rear gunner Kydd made good use of his weapons and was able to claim one Me 109 destroyed, and a further one damaged—a handsome harvest for a crew which, with all their fellows blasted from the sky, must have had the cards stacked against them.

Back at the Bight, the heat of battle slowly died down until, some half an hour after the first engagements, and as the enemy fighters' attacks slowly fell off, the remnants of the formation that had set off on the unseasonably bright and cloudless morning, had time to take stock of the situation. Wing Cdr Kellett's formation had dwindled to three—his own *OJ-D*, and *OJ-A* and *OJ-F*, flown by F/O Turner and Riddlesworth respectively—while Sqn Ldr Harris' mixed formation of Nos 149 and No 9 Squadrons seemed intact at first glance; a second revealed that at least one aircraft was having problems.

It was soon obvious that *OJ-P*, with F/O Jimmy Briden at the controls, had been hit, for from underneath the port wing there trailed a persistent plume of grey-white vapour. Steam? Ridiculous! Smoke? No, it had a 'heavier' look than that. Petrol, it had to be petrol. The fuel tank was not self-sealing, and the life-blood of the bomber was slowly but steadily ebbing away. Nor was all well with John Ramshaw's Wellington, although at the time nobody realized.

Seemingly, the first to drop into the cold water of the North Sea was *OJ-P*; ironically, if the Wimpy could have struggled on for another fifty miles or so, the crew would have landed safely at base. However, the engines died and there was nothing for it but to come down in the unfriendly ocean. Above, Harris in *N2890* saw the whole drama played out in front of him and followed the doomed bomber down as it made a successful ditching. The next thing for Harris to do was to take an accurate fix on the position. That done, the pilot ran in low over the wallowing machine and, from the rear of the starboard engine nacelle, dropped his own dinghy. As the mercy aircraft began again to make height, the men inside exchanged glances of incredulity. After all they had gone through, was yet another disaster about to occur? Their aircraft was suddenly flung into a paroxysm of vibration. Unknown to the crew, the dinghy they had dropped, which was meant to be released after ditching and not from the air, had lodged on the tailplane and was the cause of their current problem. It seemed at one point as if they were going to join Briden in the water but luckily Harris managed to stagger to the English coast and make an emergency landing at the first airfield they came across.

While this was going on, Sgt John Ramshaw and his men in *N2983* were having their own troubles. Little did they know it, but their Wellington had a holed main fuel tank on both sides. Flt Lt Peter Grant, No 1 in their 'vic' had a puncture in his port tank and had been able to transfer petrol to the other side, but for Ramshaw and his crew the outlook was grim. With no guns to operate, it fell to A/C Driver to work the emergency pump that would help to keep them aloft for a little longer. All those remaining alive had their duties in this final period of the flight home, even Ldg A/C Conolly, who had by now managed to coax the generator into giving some electrical power. The gunner toiled at the pump for a wearying half hour until the reserve tanks were dry. The motors died ... first one and then the other. The airscrews windmilled uselessly in the sudden silence, which was broken only by the sighing of the air over the battered airframe.

As altitude was lost, Ramshaw scanned the horizon while there was still the advantage of having some height over the waves. He had pre-pared his men for the worst with the announcement 'We can't make it; we'll have to land in the sea.' Now, the needle on the instrument panel counted off the Wellington's descent as it dropped from the 10,000 ft where the engines had failed. They were going down rapidly now, and the Sergeant, as his gaze swept the unfriendly water before the inevitable ditching, could hardly believe his eyes when he saw, just ahead, the welcome silhouette of a Grimsby trawler.

'I've seen a ship, and I'll try to make it!' he bellowed, as the rest of the crew braced themselves for the final impact. Good as his word, the pilot manoeuvred his stricken charge so that at the end of its glide it dropped no more than 400 yd from the trawler.

Hitting water in an aeroplane is not so very different from colliding with a solid object, and this occasion was no different. The final impact flung the pilot forward with such force that he suffered a heavy blow on the head that left him only partly conscious. Charlie Driver was among those who came out of the crash unscathed, and was able to help launch the rubber dinghy before making his own escape, along with the radio operator who had exited through the astrodome. Further forward, Ramshaw was still dazed and, after struggling out through the top of the pilot's cabin, he fell into the sea. Happily, the others managed to save him from a watery grave only moments before the Wellington put her nose down and vanished from sight below the waves.

Realizing that by now they would have been posted as missing, and that a sea search had probably been initiated by Coastal Command, the men in their little rubber craft placed all their hope in the trawler. Yet it was a full quarter of an hour before the fishermen hove in sight, and the flyers were taken aboard, there to be given hot drinks and dry clothes while the ship made for port. They landed at Grimsby at 10:00 hrs on the following day—not a moment too soon for Driver, who had suffered agonies from seasickness throughout the trip!

The so-called 'Battle of Heligoland Bight' had cost the RAF dear. Of the total of twenty-two Wellingtons that had flown over the target on the previous day, twelve had been hit by the Messerschmitts, and only two of the twelve, Sgt Ramshaw's *WS-G* and F/O Briden's *OJ-P*—both from Harris' formation—had managed to limp back and ditch in English waters.

But on the bonus side, the action was to see the award of a Distinguished Flying Cross for Kellett, two mentions in dispatches and a Distinguished Flying Medal each for A/C1 James John Mullineaux—tail gunner in Harris' *N2980*, and A/C1 Charles Ronald Driver. The telegram announcing Driver's award arrived at his parents' home where he was spending three days leave after the action in which he might so easily have died. Later he was to be re-mustered, firstly as an airframe fitter and then as an official air gunner.

* * *

The RAF had entered the war with six squadrons of Wellington bombers, six of Handley Page Hampdens and five of Armstrong Whitworth Whitleys, although the latter were regarded as obsolescent. Unlike the Nazi Luftwaffe which had seized the chance to test out its equipment in the Spanish Civil War, Great Britain had enjoyed no such opportunity, so that its bomber force was untried against a strong enemy.

However, the three attacks against Nazi shipping off Heligoland in December 1939, of which Sqn Ldr (Acting Wing Cdr) Richard Kellett had led the last two, had seemed to prove the vulnerability of unescorted bombers operating by daylight. Although champions of the mutual protection theory were able to point to the fact that the losses in the 149 and 149/9 Squadron Flights—those which had maintained the tightest formations—were proportionately small, there was no gainsaying the fact that, in the broader view, the Messerschmitts had taken a dreadful toll. This contributed to the decision to abandon Bomber Command's daytime activities, and daylight raids were not resumed until April 1940. But of all this the general public was to know nothing, as the media were for the most part agog with the news that, only the day before the Heligoland raid of 18 December, the Nazi pocket-battleship *Admiral Graf Spee* had been scuttled in the Estuary of the River Plate outside Montevideo Harbour.

* * *

April 1940—the tragedy of the Dunkirk evacuation, the humiliation of France and the ignominy of Belgium still lay in the future. The attention of the world was now focused on the Nazi invasion of Norway and Denmark, and on 23 April the gloom on the Home Front was deepened by the announcement that the Chancellor of the Exchequer had raised Income Tax to 7s 6d (38p) in the pound. Despite sombre acceptance of the new twists of fate, the British were determined to strike the enemy wherever possible, and the only instruments for such blows at that time were the machines of Bomber Command.

It was exactly 22:20 hrs on Thursday 25 April when Wellington *P9427* was lifted by P/O Swift from the darkened airfield at Mildenhall, the base of No 149 Squadron since 1937. Michael Sherwood was Swift's second pilot, and the machine was to fly No 3 in one of the 'vics' that made up the bombing force setting course for Stavanger. The Norwegian port had fallen to the Nazi invaders when 'Operation *Weserübung Nord*' had been suddenly unleashed sixteen days before, with six regiments and 1,000 aircraft. Not that this was the first air attack on the Norwegian city since its fall, for, on 14 April, the RAF had bombed Stavanger-Sola airfield and the seaplanes that had been discovered moored in Hafrs Fiord.

The decision to mount this late April attack had been taken suddenly, so suddenly in fact, that aboard *P9247*, Sgt Wood the navigator was only just getting used to the fact that he was en route for a target in occupied Norway, when he had been under the impression that he was to have the night off! In another way also, this raid was to be different, for the old theories of the advantages of mutual protection for bombers flying in formation had not been entirely disproved by the fiascos of the war's early daylight raids. On this occasion, No 149's Wellingtons had been the focal point of a frenzy of activity by ground staff during the previous hours. Each machine was now fitted with blue lamps at the wing tips so that the pilots could keep formation and thus protect each other.

At first all went well, for the night promised to be clear, and there was no likelihood of meeting the enemy so near base. The Wellington's defenders such as P/O Swift's front gunner, Cpl Collinson and his colleague at the rear, A/C Grady, had little to occupy them other than watching the adjacent blue lights.

The light cloud that had now appeared slid in wraith-like wisps over the wing surfaces and then streamed out from the trailing edges before breaking free, as if reluctant to leave the aircraft. It was not long before these vapours seemed to become denser and merged into masses. The Wellington was still only a short distance from the leader, F/O H.M. Robertson's *P9274*, but in the No 2 Wimpy it became increasingly difficult to keep the other aircraft's lights in view.

The three machines of the section had taken off at different times: Robertson first at 22:10 hrs; followed five minutes later by P/O Birch, scheduled to fly No 3 in *N3013*; and last away was *P9247* with P/O J.F. Swift at the controls, and P/O Sherwood as his co-pilot. Now their main concern was keeping the all-important blue lamps in sight. These seemed to wink as the gathering cloud intermittently obscured them at first, but then they vanished for longer periods until it was impossible to use them as guides for formation-keeping.

Only forty miles from the coast, Robertson had to make a decision —to carry on trying to hold formation by means of the lights, or to allow the three aircraft to fly to the target at Stavanger separately. Bad weather made the decision for him and the formation broke up. Michael Sherwood, who flew in No 2, confirms this development: 'Very close to Mildenhall we got into cloud and that was the last we saw of any formation.'

Alone now, the leader pressed on, and after flying on dead reckoning for two hours and fifty minutes, Robertson spotted the wavering beams of searchlights penetrating the cloud below and assumed that he was over the target. The rulebook made his next duty the positive identification of the target, but the carpet of cloud that had been below them since Mildenhall where they landed at 04:45, more than six and a half hours after take-off.

Meanwhile, P/O Birch had experienced even worse luck, for the weather was such that he was back at base and waiting for his leader at 02:55, not knowing what had happened to his companions.

Last of the three was the Swift–Sherwood team in *P9247*. Aware of the danger in attempting to search for the others, they had decided to continue the journey alone and, with a warning over the intercom for the gunners to keep a sharp lookout, they set course for Stavanger.

The crew had little idea that they were in for a wearisome night, made long by frustration. Stavanger seemed to be hiding that night. Worried that they might be using too much fuel, they kept a close eye on the flickering, silver-green luminous needles of the petrol gauges. Yet still Stavanger aerodrome remained elusive. Exactly a month to the day later, the same aircraft with the same crew was to cut matters a little too finely, so that they had to refuel at Le Bourget on the way home. On this first trip they were more cautious. Stavanger was not to be found, so the only sensible decision was to begin the long, grim, cold journey home, with the boredom broken only by the jettisoning of their bombload at Lakenheath.

Another unit familiar with the formation-keeping lights was the RAAF's 458 Squadron which arrived direct from Australia and became operational at Holme-on-Spalding Moor, South Yorkshire in November 1941. Here the lamps, remembered as 'small purple lenses', were the electricians' responsibility, together with all the other electrics in a Wimpy. Wellingtons boasted a prodigious amount of electrical equipment: the navigation and formation lights, interior illumination, plus that for the turrets and gun sights, the landing lamps, pitot head heater, the intercom system, bomb gear for sixteen racks and bombsight, undercarriage warning light, fuel and temperature gauges, plus the flotation gear and such larger items as the generators, starter motors and airscrew motors, all of which would be taken off the aircraft, stripped, cleaned and tested in the workshops, while internal wiring was being looked over on the actual airframe.*

The Wellington wiring system was peculiar to the type and was known as the 'loom' method. On paper it was good, but in practice it was not easy to maintain, since it called for a number of internal junction boxes where the ten loom wires were inter-connected. Certainly the system had the advantage that a damaged section of wiring could be quickly replaced but, since the boxes were put in as the aircraft was built, they were often inaccessible. For example, if a loom had been nicked by shrapnel, it was sometimes necessary to begin at the front of the machine and work through to the rear to trace the short-circuit. This could mean days of groping among the copper braids which had a tendency to break if not properly soldered. Such repairs were a real bugbear for the electricians who also had to carry out the daily inspections, as well as those required after every forty flying hours, and major overhauls every 360 hours. Then there were the duties of running the accumulator charging rooms, manning the pair of 3 kW Chance lights on the aerodrome, laying out telephone cables for the control cabin and the 6 W Glim lamps that went with it beside the runway, and possibly making the final connections of sea mines, if these were being carried. Quite apart from all this, early 1942 also saw Wellingtons being specially wired so that they could carry and drop poison gas, although this facility was never used. Being an electrician was certainly not a rest cure!

* * *

During the early days of the war, Wellington crews had found night navigation a problem, as peace-time training had concentrated on map reading, wind direction and force, coupled with plotting. Radio aids were available, but were scorned by some navigators who would boast of being able to tell a pilot to break cloud at a pre-determined time with complete certainty that the aerodrome would be underneath. Indeed there were cases of senior navigators being so scornful of radio aids that bearings passed by wireless operators were ignored, and pilots could well end up 100 miles off course with Snowdon unexpectedly appearing below!

It was quite a performance for the front gunner of a Wellington to get to and from his position encumbered by his flying clothing

*The vital work of cleaning the sparking plugs for the Wimpy's motors was, on the other hand, entirely the responsibility of WAAFs, in No 458 Squadron at least. By January 1942, when the squadron had ceased to be a bomber unit, the girls must have dealt with thousands of plugs.

in order to use the toilet facilities in the rear of the machine. Consequently, more than one carried a small can into which he might more conveniently relieve himself. One night a returning bomber carried a navigator who was in the habit of rejecting all bearings offered by the radio operator adding in his scorn, 'I can map-read and am looking at a river I know well', as he compared his chart with the panorama laid out below him through the bomb aimer's window.

Now the navigator did not know at this stage that the front gunner had used his important little can in the manner described. Still less did he know that the can had proved inconveniently small on this occasion and had overflowed, a streak of urine having trickled across the bomb aimer's window before freezing there. The fact that realization had dawned was indicated by a scream from the navigator as he recognized his familiar 'river' for what it was with a frustrated yell of 'I'm following a streak of piss!'

Navigational problems such as these were especially dangerous for bombers returning from raids over enemy territory for they could send an aircraft into a balloon barrage. One wireless operator remembers, having switched on the IFF (identification, friend or foe), receiving two warnings that they were on course for one of these hazards, only to be told not to worry as the navigator was in the second pilot's position, map-reading despite the dark.

'Suddenly', recalls the wireless operator, 'the aircraft shuddered, all the lights went out, and the engines screamed as we plunged into a dive.' An eternity then passed before there was a second shudder accompanied by the lights once again coming on, indicating that the remarkable pilot, Sgt Coleman, had the Wellington under control again and had brought it out of the dive.

As the over-late cries of 'Balloons!' from the crew died away, Coleman turned the aircraft through 360 degrees to fly away from the cables. At least one of the RAF men waited apprehensively as they manoeuvred to get out of the barrage and set a new course for base... this time with the aid of radio bearings!

They arrived home without further incident, the bomber seeming to fly normally. However, the landing approach proved otherwise, for hardly had the machine touched down along the illuminated flare path, when a violent swing caused the ground crew to scatter in confusion. A balloon cable had severed the controls to one engine, but the skilled pilot was ready for this, and immediately opened up the other motor to correct the swing. He finally managed to stop the aircraft, but not the rogue engine, so that the crew had finally to leap clear. The bomber continued its drunken circling until the petrol supply was cut off, and the emergency was at an end. How close the crew had come to death was discovered when examination revealed that the cable had sliced three-quarters of the way through the wing before snapping.

✭ ✭ ✭

Night operations such as these were now part of the long, hard slog that was Bomber Command's offensive against Nazi Germany, with Wellingtons as its mainstay. The enemy was in virtually complete control of Europe after the retreat from France, to which the British Expeditionary Force had sailed in 1939. The whole platform and concept of the war had changed in the early summer of 1940 with Wellingtons being sent by daylight to bomb 'targets of opportunity' on enemy concentrations. It was almost a relief to fly over these as a change from the murderous fire sent up by demoralized French and British troops who now loosed off at anything that flew. At home, the deterioration was reflected in hundreds of different ways, such as the English father who shook his head over his evening meal while listening to the radio news and remarked to his wife, 'I don't like that "retreat to prepared positions" they're talking about.' A little earlier his wife had observed to their grown-up daughter as they passed the sign of a local builder marked *Closed for the Duration*, 'Isn't it dreadful our men going off to the war again!'—an indication of just how close the two great conflicts seemed for those who lived through them.

To the crew of the Wellington over the northern coast of France now, the whole of Dunkirk seemed to be a lake of liquid fire that leapt and heaved in shades of yellow, white and orange, criss-crossed with the lines of streets made black when there was nothing left to burn. Large buildings appeared at first to be gaily decked with flags, so that it took a second glance to realize that the pennants were of flame.

From all this a great column of smoke rose up hundreds of feet into the sky, greasy and billowing from the burning oil tanks, standing out in sharp contrast against the polished copper of the sea as it reflected the glow of the conflagration. So solid did the smoke pillar seem that, as the pilot banked and turned south, he skirted its sinister shape.

In the continuous blaze of fire that was spread out below, it was impossible to pick out the comparative pin-prick of a muzzle-flash, or any other individual human activity. There was therefore small chance of selecting any 'targets of opportunity', and all the Wellington's crew could do was to scatter their load in what they hoped was the right direction and trust that the results might purchase a little more time for their countrymen and allies below. This done, the bombers closed their empty racks and turned for home, great cruciform silhouettes against the open furnace behind them.

*　*　*

The Messes of the bomber crews were quiet after they had returned that night. The waiting in the afternoon, the countermanded orders as news of the swiftly-changing situation in France had come in, the eventual take-off from the scorched grass that marked the beginning of one of the finest summers in living memory, the climb into the afternoon ... these had all been too great a contrast with the unexpected sights that had awaited them on the other side of the Channel. None would have admitted his innermost thoughts, but the feeling of impotence that afflicted them all was almost tangible. Small wonder that few wanted to release their pent-up tension, for their minds were too occupied with what they had seen. None was surprised with the announcement three days later that 'Operation Dynamo' was over; but hopefully missions such as these by Wellingtons and other bombers had contributed in some small measure to the success the operation was claimed to be.

Chapter 2
Victoria Cross

The worst of the anti-aircraft fire was behind them now, and the Wellington Ic from No 75 Squadron had dropped her bombs squarely on Münster. It was therefore with some satisfaction that Sqn Ldr R.P. Widdowson turned his machine, *L7818*, towards home. Certainly, home was a long way off but it was almost comforting to reflect that every mile brought the mixed crew—he was a Canadian, and the others were either English, Welsh or from New Zealand—closer to the sanctuary of Norfolk's Feltwell. They had been based at the airfield for fifteen months, since moving there in April 1940, a long distance off in time on this starry night of 7 July 1941. Not that there was any room for complacency among the men cocooned in the strong metal and fabric case that was their bomber: much could happen in the miles ahead.

However, on this particular night it seemed that luck was with them, for now they had reached the Zuider Zee which could be seen palely glinting 13,000 ft beneath them. Now all that stood between them and the welcoming English coast was the North Sea.

Suddenly, all hell seemed to break loose in the bomber. The mind-numbing bark of cannon and machine-gun fire burst on them as a Messerschmitt 110 night-fighter reared up suddenly below the rear of the Wellington and put in a generous burst of fire that raked the length of the fuselage. Sgt Evans in the front turret was wounded before the Messerschmitt banked away to avoid the reaction of the bomber's defenders, to be almost immediately swallowed up in the night.

Poised to receive the next attack, the crew of the bomber had not long to wait. In a few moments, the Messerschmitt was back again, delivering an attack that was almost an exact copy of the first. But this time the gunners were ready so that, with the ease of long practice, 19-year-old Sgt Box spun his turret and depressed his guns until the enemy was full in the sights. His fourteen months RNZAF service culminated in the moment which followed, for, as his fingers tightened on the triggers, a murderous fire seemed to engulf the front of the night-fighter. The point-blank range and the sustained burst of fire could have only one result: the Messerschmitt plummeted from the sky blazing like a torch.

The jubilation of the Wellington's crew was short-lived, for they had to turn their minds to taking stock of their position. It was far from reassuring: the hydraulic system had been blasted out of existence by the enemy fire, so that now the bomb doors hung uselessly open; the radio too was useless, as was the intercom. But worst of all was the sight that greeted them through the starboard windows where a fire had been started in the wing and the flames were being fed by the petrol from a fractured fuel pipe. As if they did not have enough problems, the engine on that side was showing signs of shaking free from the nacelle, and the vibrations could be felt throughout the airframe.

Sgt Evans' wound had been to his foot so that he was semi-immobilized. The other members of the crew now gathered on the stricken side of the Wellington and, having hacked a hole in the fuselage side, did their best to fight the fire in the wing with hand extinguishers. It did not take long to convince the men that their efforts were useless, for the liquid that should have doused the blaze vanished uselessly in the slipstream. The same fate befell the contents of their vacuum flasks, the coffee being the only other liquid left to them when the hand extinguishers were exhausted. Pilot Widdowson warned his men that there seemed little alternative to baling out.

'I'm going out on the wing!' The speaker was Sgt Ward*, a 22-year-old ex-teacher from Wanganui, who was flying as second pilot. While some of the men did their best to dissuade him from such a desperate measure, others picked up the axe to enlarge the hole which they had already cut in the side. Seeing this, Ward merely shook his head. There was no need for him to squeeze through the hole; it would be easier to clamber out through the astrodome.

---

*Sgt James Allen Ward is recalled as a very quiet man who even asked his friend, Flt Sgt Denis Sharp, to buy his VC ribbon for him. The award was celebrated on 7 August 1941 by No 75 (NZ) Squadron's throwing a party at Feltwell, although food rationing limited the menu to ham, salad, cakes, beer and tea.

Disregarding the protests of his colleagues, Ward now went forward and began to wriggle through the narrow opening. He was carrying an engine cover in the hope that he might be able to use it to smother the flames. So tight was the squeeze that he started to take off his parachute pack, but the others protested with such vigour that Ward changed his mind. Seeing that his friend was determined to go through with the scheme, Sgt Lawton, the navigator from Auckland, brought a rope from the dinghy and fastened it round Ward's waist before helping him through the narrow gap in the top of the fuselage.

In fact, the cord around the sergeant's body was really only a gesture as, if he were blown off, the aircraft itself might pose a greater threat than otherwise, but for the moment it satisfied the helpless men inside. They paid out the lifeline as, outside, the creeping, grotesque figure laboriously advanced. The Wellington was being flown by Widdowson as slowly as safety permitted, but even so the howling wind threatened to pluck Jimmy Ward from the wing like a leaf. His first efforts, therefore, were directed at kicking a foothold in the fabric of the fuselage so that he could gain a purchase.

The going on the curved surface of the centre-section was no easier; the ice-cold blast was still tearing at him. It was dark, too, for the flames gave only a fitful light, and Ward wasted a lot of energy in kicking a grip in the fabric, not knowing that he was within inches of a ready-made gap that had been ripped out by one of the Messerschmitt's shells.

It was only 3 ft down the fuselage side and the same distance across the inner wing but, even so, the New Zealander was so exhausted that it was an effort to beat at the flames in the wing fabric. Nevertheless, he put them out quite easily, but there still remained the engine fire which was being fuelled by escaping petrol. Lying full-length to present the smallest possible area to the slipstream that seemed determined to blow him off, inching outwards, and dragging the engine cover at the same time, he slowly twisted his body so that the heavy canvas could be pushed into the hole in the wing and on to the leaking pipe. Despite the bitter cold and the tearing blast, the Sergeant finally succeeded but, just as he was about to summon his reserves of strength for the return journey, he let go of the cover and it rose free.

More by luck than judgement, he managed to snatch the precious cloth before it vanished into the night. He tried again, only to have the same thing happen. This time Ward was less lucky and the engine cover, like some hideous ghost, danced a crazy measure on the wing, just out of his reach, before vanishing into the black void below. There was nothing for it now but to beat the fire out with his bare hands and, after what seemed an age, the flames subsided.

With the fire largely subdued, the painful return journey was begun. By now Jimmy was becoming disorientated and followed the pull on the lifeline like a man in a dream, as Lawton took up the slack. The trip back to the fuselage was a nightmare. Ward was exhausted beyond description but, after a journey that seemed to go on for ever, he was finally helped into the Wellington. Once out of the blast, his senses slowly returned to normal and he was able to take a look out of the window to satisfy himself that the residual fire could be safely left to burn itself out. Sure enough, there was no fabric left around the fire, and now, while James Ward tried to get some rest, Sqn Ldr Widdowson made all speed for home.

They had decided to land at the first convenient airfield but, before they could find one, it looked as though a new disaster was about to strike. Quite suddenly a great gush of fire lit up the interior of the Wellington and anxious glances were exchanged that soon turned to ones of relief: the fire died down almost as suddenly as it had appeared, indicating that the pool of petrol that had collected inside the wing and taken fire had been consumed.

Meanwhile, Sgt Mason, who was in charge of the radio and was the only Englishman on board, had managed to make a temporary repair to the instrument and had tried to inform base of their predicament. The message that the aircraft was in some sort of trouble had been heard, but the mention of a fire had been cut short as the radio failed again. It was therefore with relief that Feltwell later received news of the Wellington's uneventful emergency landing, at Newmarket. Not surprisingly, *L7818* was never to fly again, but it was announced some forty-eight hours later that Sgt James Allen Ward had been awarded the Victoria Cross. Sadly, he was not to live long to enjoy this decoration: only a few weeks later he was killed on air operations.

★ ★ ★

No 75 was a Commonwealth Squadron—the first one to be formed in Bomber Command. Although part of the Royal Air Force in its formative days, the squadron was officially transferred to the Royal New Zealand Air Force with effect from 4 April 1940, and its Wellingtons participated in the early bombing offensive against Nazi Germany. One of No 75's first missions was that of 15 May, when six Wellingtons formed part of a force of eighty aircraft sent to attack enemy industrial centres, No 75's target being oil installations in the Ruhr valley. The squadron also took part in a large attack on Berlin on the night of 25 August, when 119 bombers from several squadrons were sent to the capital.

Another early mission by No 75's Wellingtons was an abortive sortie when six bombers were detached to Salon in Southern France, preparatory to a June raid on targets in Italy. That this mission failed to materialize was entirely due to the French driving lorries and other vehicles on to the field to prevent the bombers taking off. The purpose of this extreme measure was to prevent any retaliation from the Italians. Nevertheless, the Wellington crews of No 75 Squadron quickly gained valuable operational experience. On some occasions their sorties were so eventful that the crews were only able to return to base due to the tremendous strength that Barnes Wallis' geodetic fuselage structure bestowed.

An example of this may be found in the tale of a bomber that was one of a force of eleven included in a great phalanx of machines destined for Hanover, among other targets. Flights such as these could be singularly unexciting, and best remembered for the extreme cold suffered by the crews. This one was no exception, as there was nothing to break the boredom. Only the in-built training of the men prevented the onset of complacency that would inevitably prove fatal when the night-fighters closed in.

On this occasion, the interceptors were 'late' and the machine, with a Flight Lieutenant from Invercargill in command, had dropped its bombs and course had been set for home. Suddenly the silence over the intercom was broken by the voice of the rear gunner. In his lonely station far from his friends he had spotted the tell-tale shape of another aircraft that was clearly not one of the formation. 'Enemy fighter astern, Skip!' He spun the turret a little, the better to bring his guns to bear. A few seconds later, the enemy loomed up, suddenly massive in his sights. Little sparks of tracer twinkled between the aircraft as they exchanged fire. Then in a moment the black shape had vanished into the greater darkness as the pilot side-slipped out of the way. Tense moments followed while the men waited for their attacker to return. It soon became clear that the Nazi had lost them, and the bomber crew could breathe freely once more.

'Keep your eyes peeled, there's more than one of the bastards around, I'll be bound!' The pilot's warning sounded metallic and harsh over the headphones.

'Here he comes again!' The warning shout came almost at the

same moment as the gunner again opened fire, so that the final syllable was swallowed up in a torrent of noise as he swung the rear turret, following the enemy night-fighter until its pilot broke off and side-slipped out of range.

There was a pause as the airmen waited for the Messerschmitt to return, but it seemed that once more they had got off lightly for, as the moments ticked by, the attack was not resumed. When the pilot checked among the crew for reported damage, this seemed slight and relief within the Wellington was almost tangible as the weary miles slipped by, taking them closer to home.

'Fighter!' There was only time for the single word after a long period of silence, but it was sufficient to galvanize the crew into increased vigilance. It was hardly necessary. The fresh attack was already being delivered from the beam—an approach especially favoured by the Luftwaffe interceptors since from that angle they were relatively safe from the defensive fire. Letting off a long burst as he bore in, the pilot of the Messerschmitt 110 had taken careful aim and only exposed himself to retribution as he broke away. Nevertheless, the front gunner of the bomber was able to aim a short burst at the swiftly passing enemy, silhouetted against the lighter backdrop of the night sky.

There was little need for the pilot to conduct the ritual inventory of damage sustained. That this was considerable was only too evident as he righted the machine. After each instinctive evasive action as the enemy came in again in an effort to finish off his victim, the Wellington had lost both speed and altitude. Indeed, it may well have been that it was this very effect that finally saved the New Zealand crew that night, for their attacker did not follow them down. He seemed content to settle for a probable kill, assuming that the Wellington pilot's tactics were not the reason for the aircraft's strange behaviour. Still, flyable after a fashion, the Wellington eventually made landfall at a field in East Anglia without injury to the crew. However, the trip had been completed with the undercarriage refusing to rise from its 'down' position and with bomb doors that remained stubbornly open. The latter was due to severed hydraulic lines that had resulted from cannon shells bursting inside the bomb bay in the final attack.

* * *

The damage suffered by this Wellington was similar to that sustained by another from No 75 Squadron which, piloted by Fred ('Popeye') Lucas, one of the unit's Flight commanders, had successfully dropped its bombload on Düsseldorf during a night attack, and had turned for a second run over the target to take photographs. Immediately it became the centre of attention of the defences below, and in a matter of seconds a direct hit on one of the engines also had the effect of so damaging the hydraulics that here again the bomb cell gaped and the dangling wheels refused to retract. Despite this, and the resultant loss of altitude, Lucas was able to bring his charge home after a nightmare trip that ended with the Wellington limping over the English coast at a height of no more than 500 ft with the fuel gauges registering empty tanks. Directed to a nearby field, the bomber was set gently down. Even as it completed its run and turned from the bright flarepath into the surrounding gloom, a few protesting coughs from the engines that had laboured so faithfully and for so long announced that they were about to run out of fuel.

★ ★ ★

That the structure of the Wellington was such that it could continue to fly despite the most severe damage was well known, but in addition it was not a difficult machine to fly. Indeed, as one pilot was to remember, 'it was a wonderful 'plane to handle'. It is true that it did have its little characteristics which made it rather eccentric, such as the change of trim that resulted from extending the flaps. This was particularly true of the earlier versions, although later a device was incorporated to compensate for the alteration of fore-and-aft control. It would be easy to exaggerate what was really a minor quirk into a vice; the change of trim was in fact just something that one became used to and learned to accept.

Getting into the Wellington's cockpit was an experience in itself, for access was through a shin-barking trap-door under the nose, calling for some athletic ability. When you managed to get through, the view from the dais-like pilot's position was remarkable, but pre-occupation with this soon faded once you were in the air, for in rough weather another of the Wellington's little oddities became evident: the structure *flexed* under all but the calmest conditions. Naturally, this was picked up by the controls since the fact that the control cables to the elevators moved in sympathy with the fuselage geodetics meant that the control column would wander gently fore and aft—a strange but harmless eccentricity.

Acceptance of traits of this nature quickly endeared the Wellington to its crews. They learned to trust the type implicitly, showing little or no apprehension even when, as is remembered by a ferry pilot, the fabric began to tear away from a wing.

Indeed it was qualities of this sort, which Barnes Wallis built into the design, that saved the lives of many a crew. One such instance concerned six men, once more from No 75 Squadron, who made up part of a bomber force directed against targets in the vicinity of Berlin.

At the controls of the bomber sat 23-year-old Flt Lt Frank Gill. He had flown to Berlin before and on that occasion had found himself forced down and caught in a cone of searchlight beams while the ground defences inflicted severe punishment on the Wellington. Escape, when it was finally made, was only a prelude to a horrendous journey back to base during which they almost ran out of fuel and the navigator lost his bearings.

Now, the problem was a different one, taking the form of patrols of Junkers 88Cs of the Nazi capital's *Nachtjagd-Geschwader*, so that part of Gill's mind was occupied with a mental rehearsal of the accepted means of trying to shake off a night-fighter. The manoeuvre involved a dive-climb-dive technique with the aircraft holding a steep turn starboard to port and port to starboard. Faced with this corkscrewing of their target, intercepting pilots would frequently break off the action and seek a new prey, hoping that its crew would be less alert.

Hardly had these thoughts passed through the pilot's mind when the calm call into his headphones 'Night-fighter astern' told him that the moment had come to replace theory with practice. He had half expected the attacks to come from below and probably on the beam, but now the presence of their assailant astern was confirmed by the roar of the defending guns in the rear turret. Caught squarely in the fire from the four weapons, the Junkers seemed almost to pause for a second in mid-flight, then, quite gracefully, one wing dropped and the big fighter lurched away to drop out of sight in a steepening dive towards the sea. However, the New Zealanders' elation was dampened when it was discovered that the short, but well-aimed burst of fire that the Junkers had managed to get off, had holed the port fuel tank and shot away the elevator on that side. Consequently, the machine was difficult to control. Despite this, and the resultant stresses on the remainder of the airframe, the long journey home was completed with no worse consequence than an exhausted crew—further testimony to the endurance and strength of the Barnes Wallis geodetic system of construction.

★ ★ ★

It was a night-fighter yet again that accounted for a further Wellington; this time one of a force from No 425 *'Les Alouettes'* Squadron. The aircraft had been sent from their base at Dishforth to attack Essen where the Krupps armament works were situated, on the night of Saturday 13 March 1943. It is interesting to note that this was the day after the first recorded use of Nazi Focke-Wulf 190 fighter-bombers for daylight attacks on targets in London.

As might be expected, the crew of the Wellington were Canadians. They were under the command of the pilot, Sgt Lamontagne from Montreal, a 24-year-old who had qualified as a pilot as recently as February of the previous year, and had only been assigned to the recently-formed *Alouettes* in October 1942.

The mission had, so far, been almost uneventful. There had been the usual anti-aircraft fire over the approach to the target, and the searchlights had been active, but nothing had happened to prevent this crew dropping their load accurately on target and setting course for base. They were therefore feeling pleased with their night's work when they learned from the navigator, Flt Sgt A.W. Brown, that they were crossing the border of Holland.

Quite suddenly, all hell broke loose from below and behind. A night-fighter had taken up position and was pumping lead with deadly effect into the Wellington. The rear gunner depressed his weapons as far as he could and returned the attack, but there was scarcely time to take aim before the enemy was gone, sliding from sight under the Wellington and banking away to port. The Nazi had left a fiery calling card, for the cockpit was well alight from the fusillade that had raked the bottom of the Wellington. Now the glow under the perspex canopy made the bomber a brightly-lit target should the Nazi return to administer the *coup de grâce*.

Only too aware that this could come at any moment, Flt Sgt J.A.V. Gauthier, the bomb-aimer, grabbed a fire extinguisher and attacked the blaze which rapidly died, leaving the cockpit full of stinking smoke and the occupants retching with the smell of hot metal and extinguisher fluid. But the Canadians' relief was short-lived, for the Nazi pilot had no intention of regarding his night's work as complete. Before any word of warning could be given, the enemy was there again, the cannon fire blasting into the bomber once more, rekindling the blaze in the cockpit.

The fire extinguisher ran out at this point, and Gilles Lamontagne was forced to relinquish the controls to beat at the flames with his hands. Before his efforts and those of the bomb-aimer could bear fruit their tormentor was again behind them, this time raking the rear fuselage with deadly effect. Within a matter of moments, the rear of the bomber was furiously ablaze, and the inferno made short work of the cables to the elevator controls.

'Abandon aircraft!' The Sergeant pilot felt slightly ridiculous using a phrase which seemed to come from a film or a book. Even as the crew moved to obey he was aware of calling into his microphone as an afterthought something along the lines of 'Bale out! Get out—she's a gonner!' There was a moment of panic when one of the escape hatches jammed, but Flt Sgt Brown seized an axe and hacked the offending panel open. Blessed silence surrounded the crew after the jerk and report of their individual canopies opening, while their stricken aircraft could be seen in the distance carving a blazing scimitar through the darkness as it made its last descent.

After two days of wandering in Dutch territory, the pilot was apprehended by the Gestapo, and, with Flt Sgts Brown and Gauthier, he was to drag out the next two years in various prisoner-of-war camps. Meanwhile, Flt Sgt Aumond, gunner, and Sgt Goulet, radio operator, both of whom were severely wounded, were to be repatriated for medical reasons before the end of the war. Gilles Lamontagne, on the other hand, had to wait until May 1945 for his release, by which time he had received notification of a mention in dispatches. In later years, Lamontagne was to become Canada's Minister of National Defense.

* * *

Indeed, misfortune often befell the crews of Wellington bombers some time after they had left the target area. This is further demonstrated by an event which took place a little over two years previously, in February 1941 to be exact. Since the airmanship in this incident left something to be desired, the identity of the squadron is probably best relegated to the mists of time, along with the real names of the crew-members! Suffice it to say that, following a successful mission over Nazi Germany, the Wellington in question was being flown by the second pilot, Flt Sgt 'Black'.

The bomber had suffered only minor damage from shell splinters over the target and, after the 'Mission completed' signal had been transmitted and acknowledged, 'Black' had been instructed to lose height from the present altitude of 12,500 ft, descending slowly to 5,000. A little later 'Crossing enemy coast' was sent and acknowledged. All seemed well; the navigator, confident of the position, assured the captain that they were crossing the coast at the right spot and the correct time. They were on course for the haven of the English base from which they had set out, and the second pilot began slowly to bring the Wimpy down.

It was while the six in the Wellington were looking forward to breakfast and bed that they heard the first disturbing sounds. They had become so used to the measured throb of the engines that they were no longer aware of it. But the new note was sufficiently unsettling for it to break into the background of noise, and the men exchanged questioning glances. They were flying at a little over 5,000 ft when the port engine began to surge with the force of internal explosions. With each fresh detonation, sparks burst from the exhausts, shedding an eerie light on the interior of the Wellington.

They were still losing height, as intended, and now, at 4,500 ft, Flt Lt 'Wright' took over control from the Sergeant, and at the same time instructed him to adjust the fuel cocks for a pump failure, for this was his diagnosis of the alarming behaviour of the engine. At the same time, he opened the front balance cock himself.

The recalcitrant motor was now dead, the last vestiges of power fading with the symptoms. The next step, obviously, was to get it going again as quickly as possible, since they were having to run the starboard engine at take-off power to maintain height. Normally, a windmilling airscrew would spin an engine into life, but the port engine refused to respond either to this treatment or to the attempts with the starter. There was nothing for it but to put the propeller blades into full coarse pitch, close the cooling gills and apply full rudder trim by way of compensation. The bomber was losing height rapidly now, far more rapidly than the pilot intended, but this was hardly surprising as they were now limping along at not more than 90 mph. The successful attack, the uneventful run home, the confidence of the navigator—all had seemed to presage the traditional 'happy landing'. Now it looked as though an emergency landing, most probably a ditching in the sea, was inevitable.

There had been no contact with the Wellington's base for some time, although the radio was still set to that frequency. 'Wright' immediately ordered the radio operator to call up two different airfields, but there was no response other than the gentle hiss over the headphones, indicating that nobody was picking up their messages. Their position was rapidly becoming desperate, so the pilot ordered the wireless operator to change coils on to the distress frequency. This he did, sending out an SOS before clamping down the key, but, as before, there was no answer.

The gravity of their position was all too clear to the pair in the cockpit: their altitude was something less than 300 ft—small wonder therefore that their radio messages had gone unheard—and they were still going down. This was confirmed by the W/T operator from the zeroing of the aerial ammeter each time that the trailing wire touched the water beneath. The only course open to the captain now was to order his crew to prepare to ditch. The gunners at nose and tail left their turrets, the floatation gear was operated, and the men stood by to launch the dinghy. Flt Lt 'Wright' had been at the controls for a quarter of an hour now, and it was obvious that they had only a few minutes left. There was time neither to jettison guns and ammunition, nor to dump the 250 gallons of fuel that still remained in the tanks, but at least they knew their position—about 35 miles off the English coast.

Carefully, gingerly, the pilot brought in his stricken bomber for its last landing. He had selected flaps down but kept the under-carriage retracted, so that they would land smoothly on the water. Speed was no more than 75 mph now and, at a height of some 10 ft, he stalled the machine and allowed it to settle on the sea. Only a moderate swell was running and the wind was from the west. They were fortunate that the scene was illuminated by bright moonlight for, without this, final judgement of the approach would have been much more difficult.

Landing on water is no soft option—it is little different from striking a solid surface, and the moment of impact produced near chaos in the Wellington. Sgt 'Black' suffered most. At the moment that they had stalled on to the water, he had been operating the fuel system. Unprepared for the shock of the impact he had failed to brace himself at the vital moment and had been flung bodily forward against the main spar. There was a sickening and audible crack and a searing pain in his neck: he knew at once that his collar bone had snapped.

The nose had gone under as the Wellington struck and, although the machine righted herself, the open escape hatch in the canopy had taken in plenty of water. As a result the gallant machine, tail and wings awash, floated with a wallowing motion that boded ill.

The same moment that had found the unfortunate second pilot being hurled against the spar had also found the navigator un-prepared, since he was attempting to operate the flotation equip-ment. At the last moment he had grabbed a rope for support, but the force of the landing had been such that he, like his colleague, had been flung forward. The force of the jolt dislocated his wrist yet, despite his efforts, the manual dinghy release was not operated.

Slowly, the majority of the dazed airmen who had congregated aft emerged through the astro-hatch, none of them bringing the waterproof ration containers that had been laid out at the ready on the bunk. Last to appear was the tail gunner who had been in water up to his chest. He was the wettest of the crew although none had gone under completely. Meanwhile, the pilot clambered out through the hatch in the roof of the cockpit and made his way to the starboard wing where the others had assembled.

The rubber dinghy had been automatically released by the immersion switch, but the men were dismayed to find that the craft was only partially inflated. This, they realized, was because it was leaning against the engine, and once it had been floated off, the raft gained its full pressure. The Wellington's crew embarked, only to find that they were still attached to the aircraft which looked like sinking at any moment. Sundry other lines and the wireless aerial were also entangled, but it was the work of a moment to cut these loose. Unfortunately, none of the men realized that at the same time they were losing the main ration container, distress signals and paddles.

An age seemed to pass—although it was probably no more than five minutes—before the dinghy with all the men aboard was washed free of the bomber by the tide. The last they saw of the Wellington was the high triangular fin and rudder silhouetted tall and black in the moonlight, with the water sending up little eddies of spume as it broke on the leading edge. Meanwhile the crew members took stock of their position.

Luckily, not everything had been lost with the items sent to the bottom, although their position was a grave one. All they had by way of provisions were three water bottles, each three-quarters full. For emergency equipment, they were left with a drogue which could act as a sea-anchor for the dinghy, nine leak stoppers, a topping-up pump and a canister of fluorescent dye with which they could stain the sea to mark their position for any searching rescue aircraft.

The sea is a lonely and cruel place, never more so than at night. The group of airmen—two of them injured— who had a few hours previously been flying through a hell of anti-aircraft fire to drop their bombs, were now huddled together for warmth in a minute rubber vessel. They were alone and without food in a waste of unfriendly water.

When it finally became light on the following morning, the February dawn struck them with all the sharpness of the winter's chill. Although the light kindled a little hope for the group, the weary hours spent straining their eyes for signs of possible rescue had taken their toll, and the men were less vigilant than before.

'Quiet!' The single word uttered by the front gunner concentrated the ears of all the men who, listening intently, thought they could hear the sound of aircraft engines. The radio operator looked at his watch and broke the silence with a murmured 'Seven o'clock.'

They were quite right, there could be no mistake now...not one but several aircraft could be clearly heard coming their way and, although the light was not strong, a few moments later the shapes of a pair of twin-engined monoplanes swept into view.

'Bloody Jerries!' snarled 'Black'. But he was wrong; the two were not Junkers 88s, as they had at first thought, but Bristol Blenheims. It was an excusable error, if a dangerous one, for the similarity of the two types was always being emphasized by instructors. Now, the misery of the men huddled in the small craft changed to joy as the two British machines seemed about to fly directly overhead. But their elation was dampened when the Blenheims suddenly turned away and were lost to sight.

About an hour later, the same Blenheims, or another pair, were back. The crew of the Wellington were now certain that rescue was at hand, for the sea was calm and the visibility good. In addition, the bag of dye was now trailing in the water behind the dinghy, making a broad fluorescent track, and each of the men was wearing his yellow cap. For good measure, they waved a large white scarf as the two machines passed by at no more than 1,000 ft, about a mile distant. Despite all the signs auguring a speedy rescue, the Blenheim crews gave no sign that they had spotted the airmen, even though the aircraft had twice passed over the dinghy.

Some time later, a Wellington appeared overhead. It was clear that it was on a search mission, as its pilot was obviously flying over squared reconnaissance areas. 'Wright' and his men were determined not to be overlooked this time. While a few redoubled their efforts with the white scarf, one of the gunners was busy with a small hand mirror which he had found in his pocket, trying to make it glint in the strong sun. But it was all to no avail: the Wellington swept majestically overhead in blissful ignorance, at an altitude of less than 1,000 ft and a mere 300 yd away. It was a dejected crew of marooned men who settled down as best they could to spend a second night in the cramped, bobbing rubber boat from which they seemed ordained never to escape.

As the next day dawned, a strong easterly wind sprang up, and the scarf that had proved useless as a signalling device was now pressed into service as a sail. With its aid and using their boots as paddles, they were able to make some slow progress towards the coast that could just be picked out in the distance. So they struggled on, throughout the day, seeing nothing which seemed to indicate that their presence had been reported.

The cold hours of darkness were upon them once more when, at 22:00 hrs, three ships were spotted in quick succession. As loudly as their condition would allow, 'Wright's' men hailed all three and although these calls were answered by each, it was the third that slowed down and stopped. The dinghy drifted alongside the larger vessel, and the crew assisted the exhausted airmen over the side one by one. Forty-eight hours had passed since they had abandoned the Wellington, and they were so cold and hungry that they could do little for themselves.

Their distress call had been transmitted far too late and in conditions which reduced the likelihood of its being heard while, although the Wellington was perfectly capable of flying on a single motor, their initial speed had been allowed to drop too low. They had then lost altitude to the point where it was impossible to dive and pick up sufficient speed to climb again. Fortitude, and not a little luck, had saved their lives.

Chapter 3
Frustration

Particularly in the early days of the Second World War, some bomber operations were filled not with derring-do, but with frustration. This could stem from a number of causes—engine failure, the weather, or simply an inability to find and indentify the target. However, few operations were more calculated to induce that feeling than the long journeys across Europe to deliver bundles of propaganda leaflets. These were called 'Bumphraids' or 'Bomphlets'; the former name, although of obvious derivation probably owing something to the humorous enemy agent character 'Fumph' in the popular 'ITMA' radio series.

Typical of these sorties was one carried out by a Wellington, *N3012*, attached to No 149 Squadron from Mildenhall, Suffolk. It was 2 March 1940, a month before the 'blue light' trials. The machine, flown by Sgt Goad, had taken off at 00:04 hrs for a sortie over Hamburg, its load consisting of 260 bundles of leaflets. Having gained height over Mildenhall, the crew settled down for the lengthy journey that was to keep them aloft for more than six hours, the greater part of the trip being made at a height of 15,000 ft. The night was to prove fine and clear with four tenths cloud at 1,000 ft over Hamburg, and visibility at the bomber's operating altitude ranging up to 50 miles.

When *N3012* reached the German industrial city, the expected activity never came and after the area had been identified, the bundles were dropped and scattered by the Wellington's slipstream. Untroubled by more than a few probing searchlights, Goad turned his machine for home, making a mental note to enter on his report the footnote 'No anti-aircraft fire was encountered'. The Wellington landed back at base at 06:22 hrs after an uneventful flight home.

Here, the atmosphere that greeted them was the reverse of tranquil, and the witnesses of that night's events in Suffolk had plenty to tell. Half an hour after Sergeant Goad's Wellington had taken off, *N2984* had left on a similar mission. At the controls sat F/O L.R. Field, beside his second pilot, Sgt Wiffen. Also aboard were Sgt Murdoch as observer with Ldg A/C Prior as radio operator, while A/C2s Smith and Hughson were nose and rear gunners.

The take-off was good, and the Wellington had completed a half-circuit of the aerodrome and turned into the wind when it became clear that something was amiss. Those on the ground heard the port engine cut out, while to many it seemed that the starboard motor was running at full revs. Suddenly, the machine fell into a dive, only to have its nose pulled up as the pilot regained control. At the very same moment the landing lamp was inexplicably switched on, but then the bomber stalled and seemed to drop out of the sky, crashing at Burnt Fen. It exploded on impact, killing all aboard and starting a fire that blazed out of control for several hours. It seemed a high price to pay, as someone observed, for delivering lavatory paper to the Germans. The flight had lasted exactly eleven minutes.

The strictures of the time forbade the dropping of bombs on any but the specified targets, so that, as in the case of the abortive Stavanger mission, it was expected that loads of high explosive be brought back or dumped. Bundles of propaganda papers were a different matter. Alternative targets were perfectly acceptable, as this was the early stage of the war when it was, perhaps naively , believed that the very proof of the fact that RAF machines had actually paid a visit in the night, might cause the German population to sue for peace, reminding them of Hermann Goring's boast: 'No enemy plane will fly over Reich territory'. One that did was Wellington *N2980*.

Sharp at 18:37 hrs, F/O Miers lifted his machine off the Suffolk grass, and a little later was being instructed by his navigator to steer 54°North, 06°East. The sky at their scheduled altitude was clear almost the whole way, right up to 10 miles from the target in fact, although a carpet of cloud obscured the ground. Flying as they were in a private, moonlit, cocooned world of their own, it was only too easy for the crew to relax, so the pilot called up each of his men in turn and warned them to keep alert; although at that period in the war the danger came from anti-aircraft fire than from night-fighters.

Radio silence within the Wellington meant that the sound of a voice over the intercom system gave more than one member of the crew a jolt. The voice which broke the silence was that of the navigator telling his pilot that, after some three hours in the air, they were in the vicinity of the target. At that moment, Miers was having his own problems. The cold, bright world outside was taking its toll. The pilot had been aware for some time that the movement and response of the Wellington's controls could tell only one story, namely that they were slowly but surely, becoming badly iced up. Finding a hole in the cloud carpet through which the world beneath might be identified, was now top priority.

As the Flying Officer took the machine down to rid it from its deathly fingers of ice, there was no reception from the ground gunners, no pencils of searchlight beams feeling about the sky for a victim to seize and hold in their blinding tentacles. Nothing, except for the unruffled map of Germany beneath, a quiet countryside with its towns and cities that seemed totally uninterested in the Englishmen's presence.

There was no other choice but to turn for home, as fuel was a vital consideration. As they did so, the sprawling mass of Hanover slid into view below, and it was on this city that the full load of leaflets was dropped. Duty done, the reciprocal course to that on which they had flown the outward journey was set, and the Wellington had totally lost its covering of ice by the time Germany faded into the distance behind the rear gunner's position. At 01:08, the strange journey terminated as the aircraft touched down at its home base and finally came to a halt in familiar surroundings after the bumping and jolts of the landing run. They had seen nothing of the enemy, Miers' men agreed as they clambered stiffly down from the Wellington; nothing, that is, except for a few barrage balloons that, like ridiculous misshapen map-pins, protruded from the cloud base over Cuxhaven.

But there were other forms of frustration that could lie in wait for Wellington bomber crews long after they had left the target area. These could take the form not only of night-fighters and concentrations of anti-aircraft guns, but also of battle damage, mechanical failure and just simple physical exhaustion. Undoubtedly the most cruel of all were the attentions of Nemesis that waited to strike until home was in sight.

Although the situation across the Channel was swiftly deteriorating, it was the policy of Bomber Command to strike at military and industrial targets in the enemy homeland whenever possible. On this particular date, Thursday 23 May 1940, the position in France was such that British soldiers were put on half rations following the loss of supply depots, and in three days it was to become necessary to begin 'Operation Dynamo', with a resultant change in the use of the home-based RAF bombers.

Just before 22:00, the first of a formation of Wellingtons took off into the night and droned across the Suffolk countryside, setting course for their intended target. It had been exactly 21:50 hours when the first of them had taken off, one of ten which included *P9224, P9245, P9247, P9248, P9270, P9273, R3164, R3174* and *R3175*. It took three-quarters of an hour for all of the bombers to get away, the penultimate departure being that of *P9270*, commanded by Flt Lt I.D. Grant-Crawford. History does not record the events that occurred during *P9270*'s trip to the target and back, except for a note that the target was successfully found and the load of bombs duly dropped. More detailed records have now vanished, so we shall probably never know why, at 03:15 hrs on the following morning, Grant-Crawford's Wellington, having been seen by many circling its base in preparation to land, and with no radio indication of damage or injury (according to surviving records), crashed without warning at Barton Mills, Suffolk. The captain, A/C Hewitt the wireless operator, and A/C Burton one of the gunners, all sustained injuries from which they subsequently died.

★ ★ ★

It was not always in the heat of battle that the wastage of war was clearly evident, nor in the results of conflict. Frequently it was apparent in more prosaic activities, such as training, as is illustrated by the tale of another Wellington that had fought a good fight in the opening days of World War 2.

Monday 18 December 1939 has passed into history as the day of the Battle of Heligoland Bight, the day when the Nazi Luftwaffe dealt so devastatingly with the Wellington daylight raiders led by Wing Cdr Kellett. Academics remember the date also for the fact that this was the first recorded instance of a Luftwaffe *Kommandeur* using 'Freya'-type radar equipment. It was set up on the island of Wangerooge in the Frisian group to control his fighters directly in their interception of the bombers. The radar had a range of 70 miles, so that the Luftwaffe pilots could choose the time and place of their attacks. This measure had paid rich dividends when combined with the advantages of their superior speeds and equipment. The latter included 20-mm Rheinmetal Borsig cannon, which had a range of between 600 and 900 yd.

Among the Wellingtons of the joint No 9 and 149 formation had been that of the leader, Sqn Ldr Harris' *N2980*. His was one of the luckier ones that had returned home, for companions *OJ-P* (F/O Briden's *N2961*) and *WG-S* (Sgt Ramshaw's *N2983*) had both had to be ditched. Harris eventually made landfall over Coltishall at 16:00 hrs.

Since that time, *N2980*, otherwise 'R for Robert', had taken part in five assaults against the enemy, only one of which was by daylight. The others were a 'Bumphlet' (Nickel) raid on Hanover, a so-called security patrol to Borkum, and the important attack on Aachen of 15 May 1940 that is generally regarded as marking the beginning of strategic bombing. Three nights later the night attack on the bridges over the Meuse at Namur was not only to be the last use of 'R for Robert' by No 149 Squadron, but would also reflect the change in tempo of Britain's war. Now, every effort was being expended to reverse the situation that had brought the British Expeditionary Force's retreat to the French beaches. At the end of the same month, *N2980* was passed to No 37 Squadron at Feltwell. As it happened, this was the third squadron that participated in the disastrous Heligoland attack. That tragic day was to result in a ban being placed on Wellingtons approaching the shores of Germany during the hours of daylight, and in the decision to fit them with self-sealing fuel tanks and augmented armour.

With its new squadron, 'R for Robert' was to take part in a further seven attacks, all with different pilots, and thus amassed a total of fourteen missions which exceeded the average operational 'life' of an RAF bomber of the period. The final sortie was a pointer to *N2980*'s fate: on 27 August 1940, the Wellington set off to attack an aircraft works at Frankfurt, but had to return to base after engine trouble was experienced. On Sunday 6 October—the same day that the weather gave London a brief respite in the Nazi Blitzkrieg, 'R for Robert' was passed to No 20 Operational Training Unit at Lossiemouth, Scotland, to join its collection of old, war-weary Wellingtons earmarked for the instruction of trainee navigators.

The time was 15:00 hrs on New Year's Eve, 1940. In the fading light that comes early to that part of Scotland in winter, *N2980*, still known by its old identity of 'R for Robert', sped down the runway and took off into the gloom with its cargo of would-be navigators. At the controls sat Sqn Ldr Nigel Marwood-Elton with, at his side, the co-pilot, PO Slater. A south-westerly course was set for Fort Augustus, where they were to turn west for the island of Canna, until a change of course north-east would head them on the last leg of a triangular route to bring them back to Lossiemouth.

They had been flying for a little under twenty minutes. The motors, from which they were separated only by the thin, vibrating fabric over the lattice of the metal geodetics, were giving forth the reassuring rumble of good-natured sewing machines. The first sign of trouble came in the shape of a snowstorm. At first it was little more than a few large, whirling flakes, but in a short space of time it became more serious, and the white mass formed what seemed to be a solid curtain through which the gallant old bomber had to battle. Pilot and co-pilot said nothing. All their attention was concentrated on the instruments, for these were the only reassuring objects in view—even the Monadhliath Mountains, that had been visible moments before, had now vanished in the all-consuming whiteness.

Then the spluttering began. At first it might have passed as a trick of the imagination, but when the eyes of the two men in front met, each realized that the other had heard it too. A matter of seconds passed before it came again. There could be no mistake now; the starboard motor went into a spasm of coughs, before, with a final splutter, it seemed to clear itself and ran as sweetly as ever.

It was the turn of the six men inside to exchange glances. P/O Lucton and Sgts Chandler, Fensome, Ford, Little and Wright all realized that they were breathing a little easier now that the danger seemed to have passed; a forced landing in a Scottish winter was a prospect no sane man would relish.

Only seconds of precious trouble-free noise had gone by before the note of the starboard Pegasus changed again. There could be no question now: a renewed spasm of coughs indicated that the motor was in its death-throes and, with a final burst of erratic running sending out tongues of flame into the heavy weather, the motor finally fell silent.

The Wellington was, of course, capable of flying on a single motor, but not under the conditions that now faced the occupants of 'R for Robert'. The gaps in the cloud that had allowed them to pick out the odd glimpse of the mountains 8,000 ft below had now closed themselves. There was only one sensible decision to be made, and the captain came to it quickly. 'Bale out!' The voice in the headphones of the six trainees was as calm and unflurried as ever, and in a moment they had all obeyed, leaving only the pilot and his assistant seated forward in the empty bomber. Unknown to them, Sgt Fensome had at that moment pulled the ripcord of his parachute too soon. The canopy had opened against the Wellington and had been sufficiently damaged to prevent it deploying properly. Its wearer plummeted helplessly to his death.

Below the bomber now ran the length of Loch Ness, 25 miles from north to south with a depth of 750 ft—greater than that of the North

Sea. This stretch of water, peaty near the bottom, has been described as 'one of the most mysterious in the world'. There was nowhere they could bring the bomber down on dry land, so the pilot decided to ditch in the loch, although the sudden snow squalls were beginning to diminish as *N2980* gradually lost height.

Landing on water, although spectacular, is never easy nor comfortable, and this occasion was no exception. The Squadron Leader brought his machine in steadily, with his port engine the single source of power. The ditching was of the 'text book' variety—smoothly, almost delicately, the old bomber came in for her last landing. At the moment of impact, the aircraft suffered the inevitable deceleration, but so well had the final moment been set up that the impact was reduced to the minimum. However, the shock was enough for the two men aboard to be flung violently forward so that their safety harness bit painfully into their flesh despite the thick flying clothing, while outside the still-spinning airscrew tossed up a huge plume of spray as it dug into the watery surface.

Then suddenly it was all over. For a split second a great quiet descended, but even in that moment Marwood-Elton and Slater realized that 'R for Robert' was beginning to settle. Slipping free from their harness and opening the escape hatch in the roof above them, they scrambled out, and half walking, half crawling, gained the starboard centre-section. The rubber dinghy, released automatically on impact, bobbed, inflated and ready for the two men, so that it took them only a short time to clamber in and paddle themselves across the freezing water to the shore.

The engine trouble that had ended the flying life of the veteran of the Heligoland engagement had started only fourteen minutes after leaving Lossiemouth. Six minutes later found her in the unfriendly waters of the loch. Now Fate was allowing her only ninety seconds in which to die. As they made their grotesque, bobbing way to the bank, some instinct made the pilot look back. There she was—'she' despite her 'R for Robert' call sign—a gaunt, black silhouette against the blacker night, the stark triangular outline of the tail fin and rudder still standing proud above the water. Then the silhouette seemed to diminish in height as the fuselage filled with the water in which she lay. Slowly, almost reluctantly, the Wellington vanished from sight with no more than a hollow splashing and a flurry of foam for ther epitaph. A half-forgotten phrase, 'hidden away for all time', sprang to the mind of Marwood-Elton as 'R-Robert' settled beneath 280 ft of water.* Here she was to lie until discovery by a team hunting the

*'Ditching' in water normally activated a hydrostatic switch which inflated buoyancy bags in the bomb cell. These could be relied upon to keep a Wellington afloat for a reasonable time in normal conditions.

legendary monster of the loch in 1977 and subsequent salvage in September 1985. (When she broke surface again, she was in such good condition that her last code, *OJ-R*, could still be made out.) Meanwhile the two pilots, after watching the disappearance of their machine, clambered up the steep bank of the loch, walked the short distance to the main A82 road and thumbed a lift from a passing lorry to Inverness.

★ ★ ★

Frustration could, indeed, plague aircrews in many different situations and must have been a common emotion in the build-up to the great raid of Sunday 31 May 1942. One thousand bombers were scheduled to fly on Cologne and, in order to find sufficient aircraft, sources outside Bomber Command had to be tapped. The response was encouraging but, almost at the eleventh hour, the promised total of 250 from Coastal Command was withdrawn due to the nature of the raid. There were no soothing euphemisms about military or industrial targets; a city—with all its inhabitants—was earmarked for destruction. While the final decision was being made as to whether Hamburg or Cologne would be the victim, behind-the-scenes activity struggled to make good the deficiency created by the Coastal Command withdrawal. Two hundred more bombers were still needed and they could not be plucked out of thin air. Reluctantly, 'Bert' Harris, in consultation with his senior air staff officer, Air Vice-Marshal Robert Saundby, decided to bring in the pupil/ instructor crews from the Operational Training Units.

Among these was Jack Paul, who had returned to Harwell from his honeymoon only six days before the raid. Jack was more familiar with small-scale operations in the Middle East and found the blazing city of Cologne an almost hypnotic sight. The old Cathedral city had been chosen instead of Hamburg because the latter would have put the raiders beyond the 300-mile range of their Gee radio aid. Now, as the pilot of one of the 1,046 bombers —a total that included four Flying Training Command Wellingtons—despatched on 'Operation Millennium', Jack Paul could hardly take his eyes from the holocaust below. The OTU machines had been sent in late in the attack, well after the incendiary force which had opened the assault. This incendiary vanguard had been given fifteen minutes to themselves to get the city alight before the remainder of the attackers arrived at 01:10 hrs.

Even from a height of 1,000 ft, it was as though he were viewing the city spread out below through red lenses. As Jack swung in from the south-east, he could easily pick out the two main bridges and the cathedral, all bathed in a lurid glow. It was towards a patch, still seemingly untouched, that the bomb-aimer was directing him.

At that moment, an urgent yell came over the crew's headphones: 'Aircraft coming up behind us!' In the tight-packed air over the target there was no way of telling whether they were dealing with friend or foe. The truth was revealed within seconds as a burst of cannon fire smashed into the fuselage on the rear port quarter, before the interceptor broke away, leaving only the flapping fabric and a stench of cordite to indicate that he had ever existed.

Gingerly, Jack Paul tested the controls, and was unable to suppress a sigh of relief when they showed no sign of damage. The same could not be said for the intercom system, however, for when he called up the crew to discover how they had fared, there were no answers. A chill shiver ran down Jack's spine. Few fighters delivered just one attack and, when the enemy came in again, the other men would not be able to let him know or advise him on evasive action.

So, he obeyed his flyer's impulses and swung the Wellington's nose to port, at the same time pulling it up. This manoeuvre presented him with a fleeting glimpse of the Messerschmitt 110 sliding by underneath, a black outline against the ruby light. Pupil gunner McCormick in the front turret enthusiastically let fly a burst from his guns, but sadly did no damage, to judge from the way that the two-seater slipped from view.

It was only a matter of moments before the second act began in the small-scale drama that was being staged above the greater one below. The enemy fighter closed in for a second attack, and it was during this that the instructor in the pilot's seat noticed that there was no answering bark from the guns in the rear turret. The first onslaught had done more damage than Jack had realized, for the tail position, manned by veteran gunner 'Bunny' Evans, had been completely put out of action. Evans was burning with frustration, unable to hit back at the night-fighter and also unable to tell his captain what had happened.

Then came the fighter's third attack. The Luftwaffe pilot hung on until the last moment before squeezing the teat, to make sure of his victim…and his aim was good. The shells struck home where they would do most damage, pounding into the wing and engine on the port side. The port engine suddenly exploded with light, sending back a banner of flame along the Wellington's fuselage.

Right up to the moment when he had to break away to avoid collision, the Nazi kept firing into the fuselage, raking through the position occupied by the radio operator, Tommy Lyons, who silently crumpled over his instruments.

Realizing that his Wellington was done for, Jack Paul hammered on the metal of the fuselage behind him with a gloved fist. The navigator looked up with a questioning expression on his face, and Paul shouted with all his might, ordering that the front gunner be told to jump before the remainder of the crew took to their parachutes as well. But, before they could all abandon the Wellington the Messerschmitt was back again to make good his kill. He came in a shallow dive with forward guns blazing and, as the Luftwaffe machine turned away, the Wellington itself began to dive, rocking as it did so.

Although the angle was none too steep at first, Paul just could not bring the nose up, so he bent forward to disconnect his radio and oxygen plugs before obeying his own order. The captain's position seemed to be empty when Bunny, the rear gunner, crawled from his useless turret and looked the length of the fuselage. In fact, Paul had lost consciousness as he bent down, and was still in his seat. However, Bunny had no time to check and, clipping on his parachute, he kicked his way through the rear escape hatch and flung himself into the fiery night.

The rear gunner's landing was hardly stylish. Happily, he escaped the furnace of Cologne: it was several miles away by now, although the glow could be seen from the Belgian border over which the final phase of the engagement had taken place. Bunny actually ended up in an apple tree in the back garden of a miner's home near Charleroi. Luckily for him, he was extracted by the local people and handed over to the Belgian resistance who, in a matter of some twelve weeks, had smuggled Bunny Evans out through France, Spain and Gibraltar. Thereafter, that apple tree was referred to as 'the Tommy Tree' by the locals.

Meanwhile, the Wellington was in the final stages of its faltering death-dive at the end of which it ploughed into the side of a house in a neighbouring village. The impact not only demolished one side of the building, but also flung out the unconscious form of Jack Paul into the rubble. The maimed Wellington then shot across the road and into an orchard where the trees finally brought it to a halt, and where it burned out.

The pilot, more used to the stresses of instruction of late than the dangers of action, knew little or nothing of his aircraft's fate. Tossed into the ruins of the cottage, he was only half-conscious, although some remaining instinct for self-preservation drove him to crawl away from the wreckage which the doomed bomber had ignited. Paul now groped in a daze through the ruins towards a distant doorway. His conviction that he was dead was reinforced by the sight of a white-robed, bearded, snowy-haired figure, which looked at him before vanishing without a word. Unable to realize that this was nothing more celestial than the tenant of the cottage roused from his bed, the RAF officer scrambled through the inviting door. He collapsed yet again once he discovered that it had taken him into the open air.

Before the Germans arrived, the pilot came to momentarily to find himself in the arms of a woman who addressed him in his own tongue. Utterly confused about how he could have reached England, as he believed this country to be, he handed his papers over to the lady, then gave up the unequal struggle and slipped back into the safe haven of unconsciousness. It was not until he was being loaded into an ambulance that the mists finally cleared, and he was taken to the hospital at Charleroi and the next day was operated on for the injuries which he had sustained. But even here a couple of surprises awaited him. The first was delivered by a 'nurse'—in fact the same woman who had succoured him in the garden—who offered to send a message to his wife. The second surprise came when he was passed a scrap of cigarette paper bearing a note signed by Bunny Evans assuring his captain that he was safe.

The other three members of the Wellington's crew were dead, their bodies cremated in the blazing bomber as it lay in the orchard. Jack was never to see Bunny again after 1942. They wrote to each other occasionally, but eventually the day came when a letter from Jack Paul was returned with the envelope marked 'Return to sender'.

* * *

One of the most potent forms of frustration in wartime is produced when lengthy preparation and detailed organization are brought to nothing at a single stroke. One such episode, from the earliest days of the Second World War, involved the Wellington bombers of two squadrons. They were about to carry the war into the heartland of the new enemy: Italy. The Fascist dictator, Benito Mussolini, had declared war on Great Britain and her allies in the manner, as one contemporary writer put it, of 'a jackal feasting on a lion's kill', for France lay bleeding under the Nazi onslaught.

The experiences of a few RAF men flying Wellingtons during

the events immediately preceding 'Operation Dynamo' have already been told. Those on the ground, however, saw a different, though no more hopeful picture, for the final days of May saw sixty-three Allied divisions attempting to hold an enemy that 134 had failed to halt at the opening of the campaign. While the Nazis had paused to regroup during the brief respite after the Dunkirk evacuation, France was simultaneously taking all available units from the Maginot line to make a last-ditch stand that was doomed to failure.

Once the British Expeditionary Force (BEF) had been safely evacuated, the Wellingtons and other heavy bombers were re-deployed. They had been largely directed against German oil targets, but now they were thrown *en masse* against the crucial enemy lines of communication. The new offensive of 5 June had carried the Germans across the Somme in the north by the same evening, and two days later they crossed the Aisne to the south.

Meanwhile, the *Duce*'s intentions had become sufficiently clear by the end of the preceding week for the Supreme War Council to strengthen their resolve. They agreed that a declaration of war by Italy, which was now seen as inevitable, would be the signal for the industrial regions of northern Italy to become an immediate target for the RAF's bombers.

With regard to squadrons flying Whitleys, this presented no great problem, as they could make the distance after a pause to re-fuel in the Channel Islands (these did not fall to the Germans until 30 June); But the Vickers Wellingtons were a different matter, for a flight from England would mean them taking on more fuel in the Marseilles area. Consequently, plans were laid for two airfields to be prepared for 'Haddock' force—as the Italian-front Wellingtons were to be code-named. However, such was the speed of events that the force had to be ordered into existence verbally by Air Vice-Marshall Evill, Senior Air Staff Officer of the British Air Forces in France, on the afternoon of the fateful Monday, 3 June. The units, including the two bomber squadrons that were to find the Wellingtons, had to be content with no more than a warning of intent, delivered by telephone twenty-four hours earlier. Consequently, at 04:00 hrs on Tuesday 4 June, four separate road convoys moved off, divided into fast and slow units. They were made up of No 71 Wing Headquarters (previously operating Fairey Battles at the opening of the French campaign), and Nos 16 and 17 Servicing Flights, which were to jointly prepare the bases in France for the 'Haddock' force Wellingtons. On that same day the British 'advance guard' arrived in Marseilles in the form of

F/O F.A.J. Burrows. He had driven 430 miles without a break in a car borrowed from Grp Capt R.M. Field, who was to command the new force.

In the days that followed there were very few wasted minutes, let alone hours. The days of preparation were crowded with the requisitioning of billets; making arrangements to take over the Château de Richeboise, 3 km north of Salon, as headquarters for the force; a visit from Wing Cdr A.R. Combe; and dealing with the arrival of the road convoys. Then the 391 tons of fuel on the petrol supply train had to be dispersed between the two bases at Salon and Le Vallon by RAF labour. Thankfully, French workers dealt with the train which arrived simultaneously carrying 344 tons of ammunition.

It was Tuesday 11 June when the bombers finally arrived. Exactly on schedule at 14:15 hrs the first of the twelve Wellingtons came in, six each from Nos 37 and 75 Squadrons. The latter was a New Zealand unit and the first Commonwealth squadron to be formed in Bomber Command. When the final machine landed at about 16:40 hrs, 'Haddock' force was ready for war, and, not surprisingly, the first sortie was ordered for the same night.

By this time, however, France was dissolving into a state of chaos. The fighters that had been reserved to intercept the expected raiders from Italy had long since been withdrawn and were now engaged in the hopeless battle that was being waged in the north. This state of affairs was to lead to astonishing events within the French and British commands.

The last of the dozen Wellingtons had hardly touched down and the crew scrambled out, stiff after their flight from England, when the telephone in Grp Capt Field's office rang. At the other end of the line was an officer of the nearest French Bomber Group. The orders which he issued to the 'Haddock' force commander were unequivocal: 'In no circumstances are Italian targets to be attacked'.

At higher level too, much the same scene was being enacted. At 21:45 hrs General Vuillemin telephoned an astounded Air Marshal Barratt, AOC-in-C British Air Forces in France, demanding that the operation be cancelled. The Air Marshall put in a call to London, seeking advice from Winston Churchill, but to no avail. The Prime Minister had already left for France and Barratt had to be content with the opinion of General Ismay at Weygand's headquarters that the operation against Italy should go ahead.

Wearily, but with some air of satisfaction, the Air Marshall now replaced his receiver only to hear the telephone ring yet again. This time it was the bewildered Field, commander of 'Haddock' force. The two men conversed for a few minutes and then Barratt contacted Ismay again. This time, the General was distinctly abrasive. 'The French have already agreed to the operation,' he said, 'and the Whitleys have already left the Channel Islands. The Wellingtons must go as arranged.'

Understandably relieved after the sorties had been sanctioned by his superior, Grp Capt Field prepared to despatch his bombers. Even as he did so, it was the turn of his telephone to begin ringing continuously. His callers were a succession of French officials, all of whom were unanimous that the Wellingtons must not depart. Field now knew better than to comply with their demands, and a few minutes after midnight the first of the Wellingtons taxied out to the runway. Behind it, three or more were waiting their turn to taxi out, while the remainder of the force waited in the distance, ready for the off and with motors ticking over.

Near the end of the runway, feeling not a little relieved that the operation was at last going ahead, stood Philip Townsend, an officer who had been on duty from 14:00 hrs supervising the servicing of the bombers and making preparations for their departure. Everything seemed to be ready when, at 21:00 hrs, he was informed by the French orderly officer that no liaison had been arranged concerning the landing and obstruction lights. It was to take two hours before these could be switched on, due to the French practice of dismissing ground staff after darkness. Now everything had been attended to and Townsend stood with an Aircraftman holding an Aldis lamp, watching the first Wellington approach preparatory to making a 180-degree turn on to the flare path.

It had not quite reached the turning point when a service van was seen approaching at speed, bumping and lurching over the rough ground. Inside were two RAF men, one of whom began shouting something even before the vehicle had stopped. 'It's scrubbed!' he was yelling above the sound of the Wellingtons' motors, 'washed out!' Without a word, the man with the lamp looked questioningly at Townsend who simply grimaced and gave a brief nod of the head in reply. The Aircraftman raised his Aldis to eye level and began to flash out the news of the operation's cancellation to the pilots. Then, one by one, the black shapes of the bombers moved away into the shadows towards their dispersal points, where men waited to picket them for the night.

Fifty minutes later found Philip Townsend entering one of the huts on the edge of the aerodrome that made up the operational headquarters of 'Haddock' force. In one room he found Grp Capt Harrison speaking on the telephone to Group headquarters. Waiting until the conversation was finished, Townsend asked the reason for the sudden cancellation of the operation. 'Political', was all he was told before being ordered to notify the radio van of the 'cease operation'.

The D/F vehicle, used as a radio and homing device centre, was situated about three miles away on the south side of the aerodrome. Anxious to finish his work and get to bed, Philip at once set off in his Hillman van, using a public road to get there. As he drove along, he was still turning over in his mind the possible reason for the sudden cancellation of the proposed attack on Italy. What he did not know was that, as the first bomber had lumbered out, several French lorries had appeared from the shadow of the hangars. Their drivers, obviously acting on orders, stopped in such a way that the bombers could not take off. With nothing to be gained from pressing the matter to the point where blows—or even shots—might be exchanged, Field had bowed to the inevitable and called off the operation.

Seemingly, these lorries vanished as suddenly as they had appeared, and so efficiently that Townsend saw nothing of them. It was with some surprise, therefore, that Philip came upon two French military vehicles at the north end of the road, drawn up and unlit. The British officer stopped behind them to find out what was happening, and discovered the drivers and mates of both vehicles huddled in the back of the second lorry. Both sides were equally surprised by the encounter, but Townsend recovered first and, returning the Frenchmen's salutes, asked the reason for their being there. 'Seeing the Wellingtons begin to move out for take-off,' the men replied, 'we put out our lights and pulled off in order not to impede the operation.' Satisfied with this, Townsend told them that the mission had been cancelled, then went to give the same message to the crew of the D/F van. On his return trip Philip noted that the two French vehicles had gone.

It was not until the next day that he heard that the take-off had allegedly been deliberately blocked. On the same day, Grp Capt Field received a visit from French Generals Gama and Houdemon who passed on the regrets of the Préfet-Maritime's Vice-Admiral from Toulon, and those of the 3rd French Army, that the steps of the night of 11 June had had to be taken. That night, Wellingtons of the same two squadrons were once again armed, fuelled and bombed up for a raid over Italy...only to have the new mission cancelled at 17:00 hrs due to reports of bad weather which included electrical storms over the Alps. On 13 June, all twelve returned to the United Kingdom.

However, Salon aerodrome was not long vacant, for Saturday 15 June saw the arrival of a further dozen Wellington Is from 99 and 149 Squadrons. The 99 Squadron crews were especially relieved to be there as they had previously been engaged mainly in armed hunts for Nazi vessels in the North Sea and 'bumph raids'. Clearly, if these aircraft were to be used at all, operations must begin immediately, for the news was that further north the enemy had captured Verdun, and the French Army GHQ had fled from Briare on the Loire to Vichy. Eight of these fresh aircraft carried out the first offensive operation by 'Haddock' force when they raided Genoa on the night of their arrival, although only a single Wellington succeeded in locating the designated target, dropping two 500- and 250-round HE bombs and 40 incendiaries.

Despite this first blow by Wellingtons against the new enemy, the days of operations such as this were numbered. Indeed, on 16 June, as the last of the Genoa raiders returned, the commander of the force was about to discuss arrangements for the possible withdrawal of his unit. Meanwhile offensive operations by the force's Wellingtons were to continue, and that night—only hours after the new Pétain government was formed—nine of 'Haddock's' bombers, one carrying Philip Townsend as a nose gunner in place of a sick crew-member, bombed Milan in very poor weather and three Wellingtons failed to find their assigned targets.

At about 04:30 on the morning of the bombers' return, orders were received by teleprinter and confirmed by cypher for the force to be evacuated immediately. By 09:30 the aircraft were refuelled and ready to leave for the United Kingdom. Soon after the last of 'Haddock' force's Wellingtons had climbed into the June sky and their navigators set course for home, a massive explosion from the detonated bomb dump signalled the end of the venture. The missions over the Alps had severely tried the engines. In addition, there had been so many engine failures—especially with the English Whitleys—that there were rumours, albeit unfounded, that sugar had been added to the fuel.

Chapter 4
The long way home

There was nothing for it but to land, and to do so as quickly as possible. Certainly, in the god-forsaken wastes of North Africa, the prospect of what might come was by no means attractive, but with a Wellington that was incapable of remaining airborne for much longer, the skipper was left with something of a Hobson's choice.

The point of the final touch-down was just south of Tobruk— not a healthy spot for British servicemen in the early months of 1942 as it was still in enemy hands. The first attempt to free it did not take place until September of the same year with 'Operation Agreement', an assault by combined seaborne and land-based commandos which failed disastrously. But this lay in the future when the Wellington that had served its crew so well made the final landing, sending up choking clouds of swirling grey-yellow dust that rolled away towards the horizon like smoke.

Once down, the six men set about discussing how to evade capture. After a short conference they agreed to trek southwards, since it seemed unlikely that enemy patrols were particularly common in that part of the desert, while they also felt that they could put the maximum distance between themselves and the Wellington before dawn if they set off in that direction. Immediately, they made what provision they could for the journey, including removing the Wellington's water tank which they lashed to a section of ladder so that it would be easier to carry. Then they set off, and by the time that the first rays of daylight streaked the sky, the six RAF men had discovered a burnt-out truck where they could rest for the day and plan the next stage.

As they talked, the sun climbed steadily in the sky above them until the vehicle was like an oven from which they dare not emerge. The six decided that they should head towards the plateau. Duties would rotate: the all-important water tank would be carried by two men; the salvaged navigational equipment by another two; while the remaining pair rested and travelled light.

At nightfall the little group of men from the Wellington resumed their walk, trudging determinedly through the night so that, when they found another charred vehicle at first light the next morning, they had covered between twelve and fifteen miles. They found it almost impossible to sleep that day because of the stifling heat and the flies; indeed, two of the men were so exhausted when the party set off again at nightfall that they had to be excused their carrying duties.

Dawn found the six running south from Sollum to the Siwa Oasis, and here they took shelter in what had earlier been a British camp. A review of their situation revealed that the precious water supply was now becoming worryingly low, while their 'meals' of one Horlicks tablet each could not be expected to have any impact on the weakness that was pervading the entire group. In the light of these facts, the men once again considered the possibility of heading north into the perennial well area—but the majority were in favour of continuing south-east.

They made themselves as comfortable as they could and then, at about 14:30 hrs, the sound of approaching footsteps put the party on the alert. Fortunately, their visitor proved to be an Arab who, seeing that they were British, begged them to move on. He explained that the spot was regularly inspected by both the Germans and Italians. Realizing their dangerous position, but also aware that they were too weak to put much distance between the camp and themselves, the RAF men asked the Arab for some food. The man thought for a moment then, without saying a word, turned on his heel and was gone. Nothing more was seen of him until two hours later, when he reappeared as abruptly as he had vanished, bringing with him a few biscuits, and some tea and rice.

The Arab was still concerned that they might fall into enemy hands, and told them that they would be safer about three miles to the east at the well of Bir Sherferzen. He promised that he would meet them there and act as their guide, so the six set off in high spirits for the well, reaching it in the early evening. They laid down their burdens, ate the meagre food and settled down to sleep.

At dawn they took turns in keeping a look out for the Arab, but the day passed with no sign of him. Agreeing that they stood little chance of getting through without his help, they waited for a second, fruitless day. It was obvious that they would have to go it alone, so they put four gallons of water in the tank—they were too weak to carry more—and started out again at nightfall. Under cover of darkness they covered some fifteen miles, finally reaching a railway station. Some cautious investigation revealed their location as Arad.

For the next two nights they struggled on, becoming increasingly desperate when all five wells they stumbled across turned out to be dry. Their minds were made up: they must turn north towards the permanent well sector and follow the road into Bug Bug.

It was 05:45 when the six weary men crested a hill and saw the coast road below. Between this and the coast itself was a military observation post but, more importantly, they could make out what appeared to be a couple of heaps about half a mile to the west: well-mounds? Leaving the five others to make what progress they could towards the coast, the second pilot set off to investigate. No sooner had he reached his goal than a noise broke the night's silence. Yes, there it was again, that low hum...some vehicles were coming his way! He took cover; just in time to avoid being spotted by a convoy of lorries. The Wellington crew had stumbled on an overnight halt for the hundreds of Italians who were building roads.

The pilot lay in hiding for about an hour before deciding to make a dash across the highway between convoys and rejoin his colleagues. He sprinted across the road and only just had time to drop behind some low scrub, before some twenty-five trucks, laden with men, thundered past only yards away. Fortunately, the Englishman was not spotted and, when the sound of the engines had faded into the distance, he was able to link up with the others once more. As they talked about his experiences, the men decided that they should pair off if absolutely necessary so that some at least might evade capture, but otherwise they must stick together so that they could pool their rations: the Horlicks tablets plus one cupful of water each per day. At dusk they pushed on eastwards.

The crew were about six miles from Bug Bug when they spotted an unattended truck, parked just off the road. To the parched men this meant only one thing: water. Three of them crept forward, intending to drain the radiator. They were almost up to the vehicle when a soldier appeared and challenged them in Italian. Thinking swiftly, the Englishmen replied 'Barrani, Sidi Barrani', hoping to give the impression that they were troops bound in that direction. The Italian was not convinced and yelled something which brought others to the scene. The trio's only hope of escape lay in flight, so they took to their heels. Utter confusion followed:

whistles were blown, trucks started up, torches flashed and orders screamed. It was this very confusion that saved the RAF men from capture, and they were able to rejoin the others undetected. At this point, two of the Wellington crew decided to set off on their own, believing that they stood a better chance on their own...they were never seen again.

The remaining four struck out to the south for five miles, then turned due east, heading for an area said to be plentiful in water. Sure enough, in the early morning they found a well and, having refilled their water bottles, they settled down to rest. After about an hour they felt energetic enough to scout for food, but they had scarcely left when they had to fling themselves behind some bushes because a truck had appeared and was stopping at the well. A group of uniformed men carrying machine-guns jumped down, and their attention was immediately caught by the supplies and tunics which the RAF men had naturally left behind. The airmen remained in hiding for about two hours waiting for the intruders to depart, but the soldiers stayed put. In the end the quartet decided to push on. There was no hope of regaining their possessions by force, as their revolvers stood no chance against the enemy's machine-guns. so, on they walked throughout the day and night, with only a three-hour rest on the next morning. By now the four were in urgent need of food and water, and felt that their position was hopeless. Yet they were determined to carry on until they dropped, so they trudged along until dawn lightened the sky.

At last the Wellington crew, hungry, thirsty and completely exhausted, stopped to rest. Later in the day two shepherds discovered them and, on learning the airmen's nationality, rushed off to return with warm goat's milk and biscuits. Refreshed, the crew were able to continue their walk. Their luck seemed to be changing at last, for they came upon an Arab village where the inhabitants fed them magnificently. At first their hosts would not allow them to stay for fear of discovery by the Italians, but a little monetary persuasion solved that problem and the crew were allowed to sleep in the village.

The next morning, the Arabs directed them to another village, but it took two days to reach there, and the despondent quartet arrived almost helpless with hunger and exhaustion. By now, walking had become sheer torture: they were all suffering from excruciatingly painful blisters on their feet which made every step agony. Their new hosts gave the airmen water and biscuits as soon as they arrived, before taking them to hide in some thick shrubbery. Food and drink were brought to the hideout throughout the day, together with— luxury of luxuries—some cigarettes, the first the airmen had seen for days.

By handing over all their remaining Egyptian money and pleading with the Arabs throughout the day, the four men secured the services of a father and son as guides. The airmen were astonished to learn that they were due south of Sidi Barrani; proof that thirteen days' wandering had robbed them of all sense of direction. At 20:00 hrs the guides arrived, complete with a camel carrying sixteen gallons of water and some food, plus Arab robes which the crew donned before setting off.

The party headed due south, then they swung south-east, covering twenty miles in the first night. The crew's spirits rose despite exhaustion and pain, but their optimism was to receive a check one morning when they were left beside a road, while the Arabs, as was their custom, went a few miles ahead to rest.

The spot chosen by the Britishers overlooked the site of a former battle in a depression littered with abandoned trucks, but which also contained a well. At 09:30 hrs one of the crew went down for water and was staggered to see a lorry-load of Italians approaching the well. To his amazement, he went unnoticed and was able to collect two gallons of water as well as a rusty 0.303 rifle and fifteen rounds of ammunition. When he reported back, it was decided that the best strategy was to lie low until the enemy moved off. It looked as if they were in for a long wait since a dozen of the Italians had set to work salvaging parts from the wrecked vehicles. Meanwhile the soldiers' transport departed, returned later laden with tyres from another site, then made off north towards Matruh, passing close to the crew.

While this was going on, one of the RAF Sergeants had been asleep in a dug-out some little way off, oblivious to everything that had taken place. Now he awoke, stretched himself, and stood up, to be immediately spotted by an Italian who approached with his rifle at the ready. Seeing this, the other three quickly put on their Arab robes then showed themselves to the Italian who by now was some yards away. The soldier stopped in his tracks and, uncertain what to do next, just stared at them. The Englishmen beckoned, shouting 'Saida', hoping that he might come nearer so that they could overpower him and force him to call to the others that all was well.

Then, quite suddenly, the man seemed to realize that these were no Arabs. He turned with a swirl of sand under his feet and rushed, shouting, back to his comrades near the well. At once, the others took out their revolvers, not bothering to go back for the machine-guns, and sprinted up the hill, firing as they came. There was nothing for it but to run so, snatching up the precious water and rifle, the crew took to their heels. The Italians were gaining on them now...no more than 150 yd separated the two groups of men; something had to be done quickly. Realizing this, one of the crew spun round, levelled the captured rifle and fired in the direction of the twelve Italians. At this, the pursuers halted, giving just sufficient time for the party to gain another 300 yd and take cover behind a shallow ridge. Behind them they then noticed a burnt truck, no more than half a mile away in the direction from which they had come. The four men ran pell-mell for the truck, hoping that it would give them enough shelter to be able to hold off the enemy until nightfall. Luck was with them, for the soldiers had not seen them in their mad dash and could be heard for the next two hours searching the desert about half a mile away.

The crew's main fear now was that the Arab guides would grow tired of waiting for them so, cautiously, first one man, then the other three, emerged from the truck and crept to the top of the ridge. The leader could see no sign of their attackers, so he beckoned the others, and alternately crawling and running they made for the spot where the guides were supposed to be waiting—three miles away in some fairly thick scrub. Before long they found the Arabs and, after some discussion, it was decided that the RAF men would press on for about five miles and then wait for the guides to catch up at nightfall. This they did, but the Arabs had some disquieting news when the six met up, for the father and son had been interrogated first by Italians, and later by a pair of Germans in a truck. Leaving the Germans encamped by the well expecting the Arabs to return in the morning to refill their water tin, the motley party pressed on. By morning they had covered 25 miles, making their way along the ridge which, although a natural highway, was fortunately devoid of enemy troops.

It was now twenty-two days since the Wellington bomber had been forced down in the sandy waste. The Arabs assured the airmen that they were travelling in the direction of the British positions, but the going was slow and painful. Then, early in the fourth week, one of them noticed a moving cloud of dust on the horizon. They dropped on to the sand. Although anyone coming from that direction was more likely to be friendly than otherwise, the quartet were determined to be cautious. The plume of sand came steadily closer but still the men made no move.

It was difficult to see the vehicles clearly in the shimmering heat-

Above All that remained of the B.9/32 after the Martlesham crash of April 1937 (from E. B. Morgan).

Below Women fabric workers covering the front of what was probably a Wellington Mk Ia (Author's collection).

Above A pre-war formation of Wellington Mk Is of No 9 Squadron. *L4288* is in the foreground (Author's collection).

Left Two types of finish for Wellington Mk Ias of the Central Bomber Establishment, coded 'DF' (Bruce Robertson collection).

Above right A tribute to its strength — the rear of a Wellington which was still intact after a crash-landing and a fire (from Norman Didwell).

Right A clear picture of the damage to Sgt James Ward's aircraft by the end of the flight during which he earned the VC. 'A' is the shell hole and seat of the fire, 1–3 the holes kicked in the fabric, and 'B' the astrodome (Imperial War Museum).

C E Kay ★ OBE DFC.
J Ward VC.
PB Lege Lucas DFC.

75 (N.Z.) Squadron

Menu

HAM

—

SALAD

—

CAKES

—

BEER

—

TEA

—

On the occasion of the approval of the award
of the Victoria Cross
to Sgt. JAMES ALLEN WARD

7 August 1941

Left Menu signed by James Ward, VC, as well as by Cyrus Kay and 'Popeye' Lucas in 1941 (courtesy Denis Sharp).
Above To judge from the airscrew blades, this early machine is the victim of a collapsed undercart (from Norman Didwell).
Below The figure on the extreme right is hand-cranking a bomb into a Wellington rack while the two men in the foreground lend a hand (Bruce Robertson collection).

Left Mk Ic *Z8787* of No 37 Squadron seen at Landing Ground 60 in December 1941. It was lost on 14 September 1942 (Bruce Robertson collection).

Middle left An early Wellington DWI showing the large magnetic hoop used to detonate mines (Author's collection).

Bottom left L7886's remains at Holton-le-Moor, Lincs, after the crash of 20 September 1941. Note the bomb score on the fin (W/C K. H. Wallis).

Right The port engine photographed from the pilot's window showing airscrew and air intake (W/C K. H. Wallis).

Below A Wellington Mk V of No 214 Squadron which used them for sea patrol and occasionally as special transports (from Norman Didwell).

Above A fine view of Mk II *W5423* in the markings of No 12 Squadron which were retained until the end of 1942 (Bruce Robertson collection).

Below The memorial plaque at Newmarket with the airscrew blade salvaged from a Wellington of 99 Squadron (G/C J. R. Goodman).

haze but, as they drew nearer, one of the Sergeants thought that there was something familiar about them. Still the vehicles came on, bobbing and pitching like boats over the uneven surface. Then, suddenly, everything fell into place: the vehicles were obviously Bren gun carriers, their crews attired in sand-coloured uniforms, shirt sleeves rolled up and with flat steel helmets on their heads. Crazed with joy, first one of the airmen and then the other three leapt to their feet with an energy that surprised even themselves, the first ripping off his shirt and waving it aloft in his elation. Good luck and Arab guidance had brought the men from the Wellington across the path of a patrol from the forward British positions. They were safe at last.

★ ★ ★

Every Wellington crew forced to land or jump in hostile territory had a different tale to tell of their efforts to evade enemy capture. European experiences differed markedly from the African variety, as Canadian Sgt Welwood was to discover on the night of 9 November 1942. He was a wireless operator flying in 'Q for Queenie' from No 425 (*Alouette*) Squadron based at Dishforth, Yorkshire, participating in a night attack by Wellingtons on Hamburg.

So far there had been no problems: the bombs had been dropped squarely on target, and the bomber had turned for home. They were north-west of Bremen when they ran into some particularly ferocious anti-aircraft fire. The big machine bucked and lurched as the exploding shells came uncomfortably close: the gunners below knew their job only too well, and had got the aircraft's range accurately.

The pilot had little alternative to holding his course, but Sgt Welwood sat at his radio in the middle of the Wellington, wishing he was back home. Suddenly, there was a massive explosion forward—'Q for Queenie' had received a direct hit from a heavy anti-aircraft shell. Almost in the same second, another burst under the stern sent the bomber into a crazy dive which seemed fairly terminal. To make matters worse, the explosion had taken out all the lights inside the machine, making the crew's situation doubly terrifying.

Welwood called up his colleagues but, as he expected, there was no response—he was on his own. In the dark he groped frantically for his parachute: with every passing second his chances of making a safe jump diminished. At first, his fingers touched only cold metal, then, to Welwood's great relief, they closed on the rough, coarse fabric he was looking for. Quickly, he donned his parachute, then felt his way to the escape hatch. Fumbling with his hands, he found the handle and struggled to throw the panel open. Nothing happened— the hatch remained stubbornly closed. The urgency of Welwood's situation was emphasized by the screaming sound of the bomber as it plunged earthward.

The second time Welwood tried the handle, he thought he detected a little movement, although the hatch was still closed. Forcing himself to think clearly, he ran his fingers round the edge of the hatch, found a place where he could insert his fingertips, then gripped the panel and gave an almighty heave. Suddenly it came away and, without giving himself time to think twice the wireless operator slipped out of the doomed aircraft.

Welwood was so close to the ground when he pulled his ripcord, that it seemed like only a few seconds before his boots thudded into a ploughed field. He rolled over, then knelt up, striking at the central disc to release his harness. At the second attempt, the straps fell away, and he was able to gather the silk of the canopy into a manageable bundle. This done, be became aware that a bright light was illuminating the scene. Looking round, he saw the remains of 'Q for Queenie' blazing fiercely only 60 yd away. Only now did he realize how close a call it had been: had the hatch come free just a couple of seconds later, he would not have lived to tell the tale. Indeed, although he did not know it, the Canadian was the only survivor from the bomber.

Hurriedly, Welwood buried his parachute in the ground. Obviously, the light of the blazing bomber must be visible for miles, and the sooner he made himself scarce, the better. Nevertheless it was a bitterly cold night and the lure of the twinkling lights of a house in the distance was irresistible.

Cautiously, Welwood drew near to the building which, on closer inspection, proved to be a farmhouse. He had not gone far when the noise of a barking dog inside the house stopped him in his tracks. The animal sounded distinctly unfriendly so, skirting the farmhouse, the Canadian made for a cluster of outhouses nearby. In one of these he found a ladder leading to a hayloft where he made his bed for the night.

The wireless operator found it hard to get to sleep: the light from the burning aircraft was disturbing enough, but also the ammunition exploded at intervals in the heat. However, at last he fell into a troubled sleep until finally the cold of dawn awoke him. It was scarcely light when he peered through the cracks in the loft door, but he knew that this was the best time to make his getaway. After a scratch breakfast of raw potatoes, he 'borrowed' an old coat that had been left hanging on a hook. The coat was doubly useful: not only did it protect him from the bitter cold, but also it was so long and voluminous that it covered his uniform and the tops of his flying boots. With any luck, he would pass as a civilian.

During the night, Sgt Welwood had heard train whistles so he knew that there must be a railway line not too far away. He set off in what he hoped was the right direction, striding along with an assumed air of confidence. He hoped that, if he could get on a west-bound train and reach Holland, the Dutch underground would take him under their wing and eventually help him to escape to Britain. It took a series of train journeys for him even to get within walking distance of the Dutch border. The last train set him down at Leer, only a few miles from his goal. And then Welwood's luck ran out. As he hunted around the railway yard for a means of covering these final miles, the Canadian was spotted and taken prisoner. In 1963, Mr Welwood returned to the farm and his 'bed and breakfast' hayloft, then visited the graves of his colleagues at Sage, near Oldenburg. At the farm he came across part of an aluminium ammunition box from the '*Alouette*' Squadron Wellington that had forced him to chance his arm in hostile territory more than two decades earlier.

★ ★ ★

The Canadian wireless operator was one of the lucky ones who lived to revisit the scenes of their wartime experiences. However, for others the long way home was to have a bitter twist, as in the case of F/O John King, observer in a Wellington bomber of 104 Squadron that was part of an attack on Tobruk at the end of 1941.

For King, this operation had a certain special significance. He liked to think that he was not a superstitious man, but even he could not dismiss from his mind the fact that this was to be his thir-teenth mission. King reflected that it was better to be safe than sorry so, as on earlier trips, the Flying Officer entrusted his per-sonal valuables to the station Adjutant's safe keeping. If the smile that went with the remark that it was 'just in case' was a trifle strained, the Adjutant was quick to wave aside the observation with a nonchalant 'I'll be here in the morning to hand them back!'

As the Wellington took off and climbed into the evening sky, King was too busy with his duties to dwell on the 101 things that could go wrong with the mission, and it was not until the bomber was above Tobruk that his misgivings surfaced again.

He had good reason to be worried, for it seemed as though his aircraft was currently the target of every anti-aircraft gun in the area. The barrage was not just heavy; it was uncomfortably accurate, too...or was King's imagination playing tricks? The unspoken question was soon answered: hardly had the attack been completed and the aimer announced the welcome 'Bombs gone!' than the port engine came to a sudden, coughing stop. It had been silenced by a direct hit from a shell splinter that was as large as a Mess soup bowl. Worse was to come. The pilot did his best to feather the useless airscrew blades so that they would cut cleanly through the air instead of turning and thus adding to the aircraft's drag. However, after several attempts, he had to confess himself beaten. The lump of shrapnel had severed the vital cable and the propeller therefore continued to windmill, placing a heavy strain on the remaining engine.

As the bomber turned for home, all the men aboard could do was to cross their fingers and trust to luck. For a while it seemed that this was doing the trick, for the starboard engine appeared determined to prove that a Wellington *could* be flown on one engine. But then gradually it became evident that the bomber would never reach base. It was losing height steadily, almost as though the inhospitable, silent and menacing desert below were a magnet.

The doomed bomber made its belly landing in a fury of sand and stones. The six men aboard were unharmed, but they found themselves in the 'middle of nowhere', 300 miles from Alamein. It seemed a good omen that the pilot had brought them down safely, and their morale was high as they gathered to work out a plan of action. The only real chance of escape, they decided, would be to capture a solitary Nazi or Italian vehicle; one of them playing the part of a baled-out German as decoy, while the remaining five chose the right moment to leap out and overpower the enemy. So, after checking their revolvers, they settled down to wait for a potential victim.

The RAF men had been lying in wait for a day and a night without seeing any sign of life, when King and one other set off in search of water. When they got back, they discovered to their astonishment that the remaining four had vanished. Had they been rescued, or captured? The pair's musings were cut short by the sound of an approaching vehicle. Quickly, they clambered into the rear of the wrecked Wellington and waited. They could hear the car outside coming uncomfortably close to their hiding place, and the two men held their breath as they realized that the car was stopping next to the bomber. For a few seconds you could have heard a pin drop. Then an English voice that they recognized only too well broke the silence. Throwing caution to the desert winds, both men rushed into the open to behold an incredible sight: a Nazi officer and two other ranks under their colleagues' orders. Evidently, the Wellington crew had seized the chance of making a capture while the water party was away.

Their next problem was what to do with the prisoners. This was quickly solved when it was suggested that they should be left safely in the shade of the Wellington—without their boots, of course! This done, the RAF crew set off in the well-stocked Volkswagen in the direction of the Allied lines, aware that the real danger would come when they attempted to cross the lines. Consequently, they planned to abandon their vehicle within walking distance of some thinly-patrolled point as near to Alamein as possible.

The Wellington crew's journey was uneventful, apart from an inadvertent crossing of a minefield, until they hove in sight of an Arab encampment. They wondered whether to recruit a guide here, but thought better of it when they noticed that every man they saw had only a stump in place of his left hand: someone remembered that this mutilation was the accepted punishment in Arab circles for robbers or murderers, so the fugitives prudently pressed on.

With the aid of King's compass, they kept a steady course but were repeatedly disappointed when the sight of civilization seemingly just on the horizon turned out to be no more than a series of mirages. On one occasion, however, their eyes did not deceive them; unfortunately, this outpost of 'civilization' proved to be the Luftwaffe airfield at Mersa Matruh, so even this had to be avoided!

Alamein was only about 20 miles away when the front springs of the Volkswagen broke. Their failure may well have been due to the fact that the latter part of the 250-mile journey had been accomplished with the tyres stuffed with parachutes, after rough ground had caused a series of punctures. The final straw came a little later when, with a lurch, the rear axle snapped. There was nothing for it but to gather up the remaining food and water and set off on foot. Progress was painfully slow as the men had to keep stopping to empty the sand from their flying boots. Soon, the last stretch lay ahead, but between themselves and the Allied lines lay a Nazi encampment, so they decided to brazen it out, walking through at night and relying on sheer cheek to carry them through. Their brave plan did not succeed: a few hours later they were not on friendly territory but in an Italian prisoner-of-war cage eating tinned meat. The Italians refused to give the RAF men water, but luckily the two soldiers imprisoned with them shared their ration.

The next day all eight were told that they were to be sent by lorry to a permanent prison camp. With only four guards on the 200-mile journey the PoWs found it easy to devise an escape plan. At an overnight stop, while two of the sentries had slung their weapons, reassured by the seeming weariness of the prisoners, a yell of 'Now!' from the Army Sergeant flung the group into a frenzy of activity. While the NCO made a lunge at one of their jailors, the Army officer made a dive at some unattended side-arms, leaving the Wellington crew to make short work of the remaining sentries and drivers. Almost before the Italians had reacted, the tables had been turned.

Fortunately a party of Germans that passed by soon afterwards did not notice anything amiss, and shortly the Britishers set off in one of the Italian lorries, taking their captives with them. The main problem during the trip was the lack of water. The radiator boiled repeatedly since, as they had only half a can of drinking water, none could be spared for cooling the engine. Eventually, a derelict vehicle yielded some rusty water, most of which went in the radiator, leaving a little for the men. The fugitives' spirits were not raised three days after setting off when they found that the only water hole they had seen was polluted with oil.

By now the need to quench their thirst was becoming overwhelming, so John King rode on the top of the cab to keep a look-out for possible wells. Sadly, many of his sighting turned out to be yet more mirages, but at last he spotted a well where the precious liquid turned out to be just about drinkable, despite its milky appearance. Having slaked their thirst and washed off some of the dust, the party set out to cover the 90 miles that separated them from the Allies.

Just when it seemed that the worst was over, the lorry broke down and their provisions dwindled to almost nothing. The group took what shelter they could from the sun and prepared for the inevitable slow death that they knew must come. In just such spirits they were discovered by a party from the Long Range Desert Group.

Leaving the Italians with what little food remained, the British soldiers and the Wellington crew set off with their liberators for a secret hideout, where they rested for a few days before being air-lifted to safety after a radio call to the local SAS HQ.

So F/O John King was finally able to report to his Adjutant and claim back his watch and possessions. However, not every story has a happy ending: on a second tour of duty, this time in Europe, King was shot down over Holland and taken prisoner, to be held captive for the remainder of the war. He stayed with the RAF when peace came, with a permanent commission from 1 April 1952. By now his days of flying in Wellingtons were long gone, so that it was in a Lancaster, as Adjutant of No 25 Squadron, that he died in his third crash-landing.

Chapter 5
Sea patrol

Although conceived as a bomber, the Wellington soon showed that it had plenty of potential in other directions. One early wartime adaptation had been for rather unusual sea patrol duties. These were the detonation of magnetic mines using huge magnetic fields fitted to the underside of the Wellingtons. These machines were known as DWIs, a designation which was meant to imply that they carried a 'Directional Wireless Installation'.

That the new Nazi mines presented a real threat to British shipping was made only too clear on 21 November 1939 when the new cruiser HMS *Belfast* was so severely damaged by a mine of this type in the Firth of Forth that repairs kept her out of action for many months. These mines had also taken a heavy toll of merchant shipping, particularly in the Thames Estuary where U-boats had laid them almost as soon as war had been declared. There was no effective means of sweeping these, so they might lie for a considerable time on the ocean bed, waiting for the magnetic influence of a ship to fire them. These mines did not rely on contact pistols; unlike the conventional sea mine.

It came as no surprise when the Commander-in-Chief, the Nore, privately stated that, because the three main channels leading to the Port of London had been sown with the new weapon, 'the Thames was full of sunken ships'. There was now only a narrow passage which was being used by the vital colliers that supplied fuel to London's power stations.

Winston Churchill, then First Lord of the Admiralty, demanded daily progress reports supported by photographs to ensure that a maximum effort to combat the new menace was being made. Once one of the mines had been acquired intact at Shoeburyness, Vickers had been ordered by the Admiralty to convert some Wellingtons as flying minesweepers, and the first four were produced by the Experimental Department at Weybridge.

The conversion work consisted of suspending a massive ring, 49 ft 9 in in diameter, under the wing panels and beneath the rear fuselage. Within the casing, a concentrically-wound coil of fifty turns of insulated aluminium strip could be energized by a 100V generator coupled to an ordinary Ford V8 car engine in the fuselage. Despite the fact that all extraneous equipment—such as radio, gun turrets and even some fuel tanks—had been removed, the final all-up weight was little different from that of a fully-laden Wellington bomber. This state of affairs created certain problems, especially since the ring to some degree affected the control responses during landing.

After taxying trials to ensure that the massive ring would not vibrate uncontrollably when the machine began to move, the first test flight took place at Weybridge on 21 December 1939. Vickers' chief test pilot 'Mutt' Summers was at the controls and gave particular attention to the aircraft's ground behaviour: it was proposed that the operational unit should be based at Manston, Kent, an airfield which at that time had a rough surface and no concrete runways.

Summers and Barnes Wallis, the designer of the Wellington, were reasonably satisfied with the outcome of these trials, so *P2518*, the first DWI Mk I, was sent on to Boscombe Down for the installation of the generator and its equipment. This work was completed by 2 January 1940, and on the following day the first tests with this aboard were carried out with Sqn Ldr H.A.I. 'Bruin' Purvis, a brilliant pilot with naval experience, in charge. The firing mechanism from the Shoeburyness mine was set up on the ground for these trials, and connected to a flash unit that would actuate a cine-camera arranged to record the relative positions of the Wellington and the firing point. The films showed that the mine would be fired by the aircraft when it was immediately overhead and not before. This was heartening news for, as the Wellington was to make the sweep at a very low level, it had to be given sufficient time to escape the blast and dome of water that would be thrown up.

On 4 January, the first compassless flight was made to find out what navigational problems might arise, since it was obvious that magnetic compasses would have to be discarded. Indeed, the arrangements for ensuring that the first DW1 was an almost entirely magnet-free aeroplane were so painstaking that the navigator, Lt Comd A.S. Bolt—believed by many to be the originator of the aerial minesweeper concept—popped along to Bond Street to buy anti-magnetic watches for the observers.

Four days later, the first attempts were made to blow up an actual mine. The weather was none too good, with poor visibility, but such was the urgency of the new measures that the test could not be postponed. Consequently, the Wellington set course for a point about eight miles north of Margate, escorted by three Bristol Blenheim fighters. A naval photographer crouched in the nose of one of the Blenheims, equipped with a movie camera to record the event while, below, a rescue launch was standing by.

The four aircraft had taken off at 14:20 hrs but it took a little time to reach the minefield. The Wellington had a crew of three: Purvis at the controls, Bolt as navigator—although he sat up front to help locate the mined area—and Sqn Ldr John Chaplin, who was in charge and also looking after the generator.

After several runs without success, at last there was a loud bang that could be heard above the note of the engines, and the Wellington bucked. The navigator went aft to consult a recording accelerator installed by the Royal Aircraft Establishment, and noted that its needle registered 3.5g. Six further runs produced negative results and, since the visibility was deteriorating with the onset of dusk, the machine returned to base.

The news that the prototype had successfully detonated a mine was rushed to the First Lord of the Admiralty and the Headquarters at Chatham. However, further tests were halted by the onset of snow, heralding one of the most severe winters in living memory, and it was several days before the weather improved. When the Wellington took to the sky again, it made two runs over known minefields but neither produced satisfactory results.

The lack of success during the morning sortie of 13 January made the crew feel so frustrated that, when they went up for the afternoon sweep, the pilot gritted his teeth and brought the Wellington down below the decreed safety height of 35 ft. Purvis, Bolt and Chaplin were almost immediately rewarded by a massive explosion under the aircraft which blew open the entrance hatch under the nose! They continued with the same tactics, and a short while later another bang was followed by a cracking sound that could only mean that the structure of the aircraft had been damaged. In fact, the force of this explosion was so great that the crew were momentarily stunned, the hatch under the cockpit was blasted open and the cover over the dorsal exit flew off! As soon as he had recovered his wits, Sqn Ldr Chaplin switched off the generator then went aft to consult the accelerometer: it was registering 10g!

At this point, the Wellington crew wisely decided to fly sedately back to base since it seemed probable that the aircraft had suffered serious structural damage. Sqn Ldr Purvis put the machine down as gently as possible before slowly taxying to the hangar. Experts from Farnborough examined the bomber the next morning and were astonished to discover that, such was the strength of the geodetic structure, the Wellington was as sound as a bell, even though it must have been flying at well below the prescribed minimum altitude when detonation occurred.

Orders to go ahead with the conversion of further Wellingtons followed quickly, issued by no less a person than the Prime Minister Neville Chamberlain himself, spurred on by Churchill. The modifications were carried out by the Rollason Aircraft Company at Croydon, Surrey, so that Wellingtons with a 'halo' commonly perplexed spotters in the vicinity during the first part of 1940. These aircraft were designated the DW1 Mk II, since their generators were powered by de Havilland Gipsy Six aero-engines and the coils within the giant rings now consisted of more turns of thinner aluminium strip. The whole installation was in fact lighter, thanks in part to a new, streamlined and more powerful 900 kW generator that produced current at 500V. A total of twelve of these Mk IIs were built at Croydon in an atmosphere of great secrecy inside the locked sheds that made up 'D' hangar. The actual assembly of the all-important rings was done not by Rollason's regular staff, but by specialists who worked on sections of the ring supported on trestles; the last ring was produced as late as August 1942.

In addition to these aircraft, there were other Coastal Command versions, such as those fitted with powerful searchlights devised by Wing Cmdr H. de V. Leigh and subsequently known as Leigh Light Wellingtons. These were used in nocturnal U-boat hunts, pioneered by No 172 Squadron which became operational in June 1942.

The Leigh Light Wellingtons were equipped not only with the light, which was mounted in the old ventral 'dustbin' position, but also with the formidable new Torpex depth charges which detonated not far below the surface of the water. To operate this array, highly-trained crews were called for—experts in flying and operating at low level over the sea by night.

* * *

At the briefing for the first operation of this type the crews learned that take-off from the North Devon base would be at 21:00 hrs, heading for the Bishop's Rock lighthouse. There the formation would fan out, taking a route direct to Spain before flying along its coast and then back home. For patrols of this nature, extra fuel was carried in a new tank installed in the bomb bay. This meant that the Wellingtons could stay out for up to thirteen hours, although it was estimated that the average duration of such sorties would be nine hours.

'Won't we be sitting ducks when the light is turned on?' asked a gunner when the briefing concluded with the usual 'Any questions?' from the operations officer. 'Open up with your front guns,' he replied cheerfully, 'that'll make their gun crews keep their heads down!' 'Sir, we haven't got any front guns!' came the plaintive reply. There was the briefest of pauses before the ops officer came back with, 'Then keep the light in their eyes!' and a burst of laughter broke the tension. Although the men had been handpicked from the RAF Coastal Command Development Unit, they were still prey to 'first night nerves'!

They would be hunting in the dark, but the sky was still light as the four machines taxied out to the very end of Chivenor's runway. It was a calm evening but the machines were carrying 2 tons excess weight so that they would need every yard of space to get off the ground. They stood with engines roaring, straining on the brakes until the signal was given for the first one to be away. It roared forward, then struggled into the air at the last moment, to be followed by the other three in quick succession. Once airborne, the pilots selected undercarriage up, then reduced boost and revs slightly until a few hundred feet registered on the altimeter indicated that it was safe to begin a slow turn to port. Course was set along the Devon-Cornwall coast towards the Scillies and then out over the Bay of Biscay.

As the patrol continued, darkness set in, relieved only by starlight, while the beat of the engines became almost soporific.

So far, the spinning monotony of the radar screen had shown nothing to excite the operator's attention, but suddenly the blue-green pencil of light centred in the middle of the glass disc took on a new shape. 'Blip coming up ten miles ahead, Skipper! Five degrees to port!' In a moment the atmosphere became highly charged as the pilot calmly ordered 'Action stations!' The second pilot began to crawl forward so that he could guide the captain from the vantage point in the nose of the Wellington. It was no easy trip, as he had to clamber over the batteries on which the Leigh Light depended. The light was lowered, although it would not be switched on until the Wellington was one mile from the indicated position of the target. Slowly, the pilot brought his machine down, nearer the sea.

'Light on!' A great glare of blue-white light suddenly sprang from the underpart of the Wellington. Caught in the cruel beam was a small 'Tunnyman' fishing vessel with a large, white sail standing out stark and white against the blackness of the sea: a false alarm. The light was doused, and the cupola holding it was hand-pumped up into the fuselage by the navigator working the hydraulic control. The pilot pulled back lightly on the control column, the revs and boost increased as the nose came up, and the stately aircraft climbed to resume its patrol at 1,000 ft, finally returning to base, nine hours after departure.

The station was agog with excitement at the story the Flight commander had to tell of his outing. As with the first Wellington, a blip had suddenly appeared on the screen of his radar, and he had manoeuvred much as the first pilot had done. When the light was switched on, it had revealed no innocent fishing boat, but the sinister outline of a submarine on the surface. Confused by the false reading on his barometric-pressure altimeter, the pilot overshot on the first run in, but on the second attempt he could see that the submarine was sending up recognition signals. For a moment, the captain hesitated, wondering whether the display of pyrotechnics indicated that the vessel caught in his glare was friendly. Then his mind cleared: British subs burned flares on the surface. He turned ready to attack, and a stick of depth charges sent up a curtain of water as they struck home. Later the news was to come through that his aim had been good: the submarine was the Italian *Luigi Torelli* and had sustained severe damage. As a result, she dared not submerge so that, when a Short Sunderland flying boat found her the following day, she was forced to struggle to the Spanish port of Santander.

The pattern for later operations was soon established after these early sorties. However, as the weeks passed, the Wellingtons had their fair share of trouble: the overtaxed engines showed their resentment with sticking exhaust valves, and oil leaks which resulted in seized power units and broken springs. The men, too, reacted badly. This was inconclusive work, the outcome of operations was often unknown. Also they had to contend with sheer weariness, boredom, and those altimeter readings which could result in pilots and crews vanishing without trace, swallowed in a hostile sea.

But on occasion there were rewards: a U-boat might stay and attempt to fight it out, and sometimes there were even visible kills, although frequently it was a case of 'the one that got away'. A blip may have shown up a vessel only a few miles ahead, and as the light was lowered and the Wellington closed in for an attack, the navigator might have thought he saw another light burning to one side. It would be well below their own height and could not possibly come from another aircraft bent on the same hunt. Then realization would dawn—it was nothing more than the phosphorescent wake of their prey making all speed in the opposite direction. The pilot would then make a sharp 'S' turn to lose altitude and come in low where the U-boat should be, only to find nothing below save for a swirl of water where the sub crash-dived to escape the taunting light. 'Well, at least we scared him!' the crew would agree, as the lonely patrol was resumed.

In circumstances such as these, No 179 Squadron's Wellingtons sank nine U-boats and shared another with a different unit, while Nos 179 and 407 claimed seven and four kills respectively.

* * *

Much thought was given to the menace of marauding submarines. The chief hope of reducing their numbers lay in hunting from the air and the Vickers Wellington proved particularly suitable for this work. However, the unmodified Wellingtons were not being used as effectively as the Leigh Light machines, so concentrated effort went into devising special hunting methods for individual areas. It was well known that U-boats operating in the Mediterranean did so in the main singly, instead of adopting the pack tactics of the Atlantic, and this fact formed the basis of 'Operation Swamp'.

Other factors had to be taken into account by the tactical planners. For example, after making a strike, a U-boat would immediately submerge to counter the threat of reprisal, but surface again to make a quick getaway from the area and to charge the batteries. The only other options were to attempt to escape under water or, if the vessel was known to be the quarry in an aerial hunt, to keep submerged and try to outlast the endurance of the aircraft. There was a time limit to this last strategy, for a U-boat could not remain below the surface for longer than about forty-eight hours and, after the first thirty hours, the crew would be breathing stale air and the batteries would begin to run dangerously low.

The main requirement therefore was for a concentration of aircraft to swamp the area of every confirmed sighting and to maintain the search for forty-eight hours over the entire area of the U-boat's travel. An immediate problem presented itself in that there were only limited resources available in the Mediterranean. However, this was alleviated to some extent by the fact that convoys were confined to coastal routes so that, in practice, the aircraft would not have to hunt too far from land.

The first 'Operation Swamp' sorties were flown on 15 October 1943, and this and the four subsequent hunts that were flown before the end of the year gave a total of 520 flying hours. During this period there were six re-sightings of submarines, making an average of 90 hours per sighting compared to about 700 hours under the previous system. The largest 'Swamp' hunt did not take place until early in the following year. Three Lockhead Hudsons started the search, these were soon joined by Wellingtons, and eventually fifty machines were involved flying for nearly 1,000 hours in 150 sorties spread over five days.

The hunt was triggered by the sighting of a U-boat at about 00:35 hrs some thirty miles north-west of Oran. Two destroyers and a minesweeper had already been sent to the area from La Senia but, after they had searched for two and a half hours with no results, the area was extended, and four more destroyers, the Hudsons and some Latecoeres were brought in. This produced no results so, at 17:00 hrs, the field was again widened and four Leigh Light Wellingtons were called in for operation during the hours of darkness. Other Wellingtons, this time from Gibraltar, were despatched to cover the waters off the Spanish coast following reports that one, and probably more, of the suspect Nazi vessels had entered the Atlantic.

It was almost 23:30 when the monotony of night patrol was suddenly broken in Wellington 'H for Harry' by the sight of the submarine 1,500 ft below, some 15 miles east-south-east of Cape de Gata. Shortening the distance by a couple of miles, the captain then turned away and, keeping visual contact with the enemy, at four miles swung round for an attack up-moon. Five minutes later there in front of them was a 517-ton submarine travelling on the surface at some 20 kn.

Swinging round to take full advantage of the darker part of the sky, the Wellington pilot brought his aircraft in for a beam attack, steadily losing height as he did so until the machine was only 40 ft above the waves. From this low altitude eight 250-lb Torpex depth charges with Mk II Tail fuzing were released from the bomb-bay. Of these, six undershot, but the final pair sent up two mighty columns of water only 50 ft from the sub's starboard quarter and must have inflicted some damage. The Wellington was still only a mile distant when the Nazi crew recovered from their surprise and bravely opened fire. 'H for Harry' was in an ideal position so that the rear gunner was able to see his target in the full light and reply in kind, claiming hits on the conning tower before both sides broke off the action.

Having climbed to a safe altitude, the Wellington captain now circled, all the time keeping his quarry in sight and dropping sea markers. Then, quite suddenly, the U-boat was gone—vanished as if it had never existed, leaving scarcely a swirl of bubbles to show where it had crash-dived.

About a quarter of an hour later, and ten miles west of this position, another Wellington, this time 'P for Pip', was on patrol when a vessel registered on the ASV screen and the Leigh Light was switched on. There below, caught in the great beam of blue-white light was a submarine—thought at the time to be that which 'H for Harry' had attacked—on the surface with decks awash, but taking avoiding action and leaving a sharply-defined wake. Without delay, the Wellington captain brought his machine sharply round for an attack and his 250-lb depth charges exploded across the enemy's stern. But the Nazi crew below gave as good as they got, and their gunfire riddled the Wellington's port wing. The pilot reluctantly turned for Gibraltar to nurse his aircraft's wounds, but the tail gunner reported that his last sight of their target was of a submarine with its stern below the waves and its bow riding unnaturally high. The remainder of the day passed without further event other than an ASV contact at 23:40 hrs, unsupported by visual observation, which was logged by one of the six Wellingtons now in the area.

By now it was Saturday 8 January, and at 03:29 hrs one of the Gibraltar Wellingtons, 'R for Robert', made ASV contact with a target that turned out to be a U-boat lying on the surface, 1,000 ft below them. However, luck was not with the Wimpy for, as it swept overhead and turned preparatory to attacking, the vessel crash-dived. Although a long watch was maintained, with a similar aircraft fitted with a Leigh Light coming in to assist at 04:50 hrs, the enemy did not re-appear.

This, the largest of all 'Swamp' operations had now lasted something like thirty hours, during which time two hunt areas had evolved—that off Cape de Gata and the Alicante vicinity. The latter area had first been patrolled at dawn on 8 January by a pair of Leigh Light Wellingtons, which were joined by four more at 15:00 hours, with another quartet coming in later to widen the search during the night. During this time there had been little luck: at 20:42 hrs, Wellington 'Z for Zebra' reported a fading contact but nothing else. In fact, it was not until 09:25 hrs on 9 January, when five extra Wellingtons had been ordered to extend the coverage even further, that a report came in of a blue oil patch, followed by the sighting of a long brown slick little less than an hour later.

While this was going on, Hudsons had relieved the Wellingtons off Cape de Gata. Then, at 19:30 on the evening of the 8th, Vickers aircraft returned to the hunt in the form of three fitted with Leigh Lights, although in the event it was a Gibraltar Wellington, coded 'N for Nuts', that made the next contact one and three-quarter hours later.

It was bright moonlight when the pilot of 'N for Nuts' took his

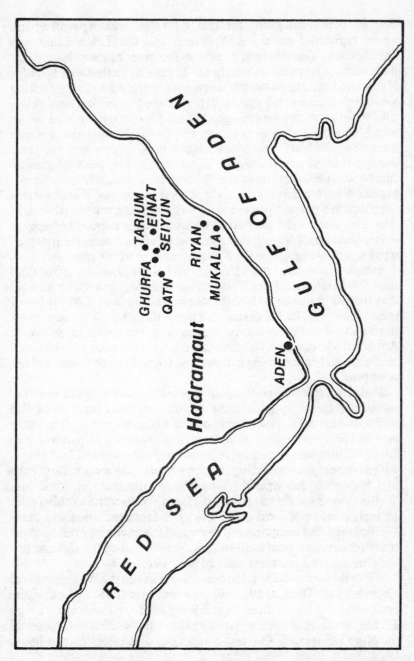

The 'Swamp' hunt of 7–12 January 1944, involving many Vickers Wellingtons.

machine down in a shallow dive to make visual confirmation of the ASV sighting, there, a mere two miles away, was an enemy submarine on the surface. Each saw the other almost simultaneously so that, while the aircraft straddled the conning tower and the rear gunner fired some 600 rounds at the U-boat, those below returned the fire with interest. Surprised that the vessel showed no inclination to dive, the Wellington pilot broke off the action and decided to shadow the enemy.

Twenty minutes passed before another, similar aircraft, reported a submarine at roughly the same position. Immediately an attack was initiated at right angles to the port beam, with depth charges being dropped from as low as 150 ft. No doubt acting on the principle of waiting until they could see the 'whites of their attackers' eyes', the sailors on the U-boat held their fire until Wellington 'Y for Yorker' was a perfect target, then let fly what seemed like a solid curtain of hot steel which the aircraft had to penetrate.

Emerging from this and taking the machine out of range, the pilot had not even had time to check on his crew when the navigator's voice came over his headphones: 'The port wing's had it!' The pilot hardly needed to be told, for most of the wing covering was ablaze, and large streamers of burning fabric were flapping in the rush of air before tearing free and spinning aft.

Every second counts at such a low altitude. 'Y for Yorker' was obviously doomed and the captain just had time to yell, 'Brace yourselves, I'll have to ditch her!' before bringing the big machine down for the smoothest crash-landing he could manage. Nevertheless, the crew were thrown about inside like loose peas in a pod, and a great curved gush of water spewed up as the aircraft struck. Luckily there were no major injuries to the four crew who were plucked from the water by a Spanish cutter. More than one of the RAF men were firmly of the opinion (although it was never confirmed) that 'Yorker's' *coup de grâce* had come not from the submarine they were attacking, but from another about half a mile away, that they had failed to notice.

Meanwhile, the sighting signal transmitted by 'Yorker's' radio operator had not gone unnoticed by 'B for Beer' and 'M for Monkey' of the same squadron, and these two Wellingtons swept in to take their revenge at 22:02 hrs. 'B' roared in first at 75 ft to deliver eight depth charges 40 ft apart, straddling the U-boat, before making its escape.

The enemy crew then enjoyed a very brief respite: for three minutes the second Wellington, 'M for Monkey', circled the area while airmen examined the sub. The vessel below had made no attempt to dive and, albeit on an even keel, was either stationary or moving very slowly, so that finishing it off seemed little more than a formality. Accordingly, 'M for Monkey' came round, levelled off and swooped in low for the final attack with another eight depth charges.

However the enemy was not going to die without a fight. As the bomber came in, the crew below threw up such a blanket of fire that it was impossible to tell whether the depth charges had hit home other than that the first certainly undershot and caused no damage. Still, the pilot thought that two had fallen about 80 ft from the hull and must have at least buckled some of the Nazi vessel's plates. Then came the news that the accuracy of the Germans' shooting had been better than expected—the Wimpy's rear gunner was now lying in a pool of his own blood on the floor of the turret, although thankfully he was still alive.

While this drama was being enacted, 'B for Beer' was not taking it easy. The pilot had taken his machine round in a great arc, all the time keeping a watchful eye on the situation. The crew's observations gave grounds for optimism, as the surface of the sea was tarnished by oil streaks about a mile long, although they were at some distance from the target vessel. Consequently, 'B for Beer' dropped marine markers to indicate what might be signs of another submarine, or perhaps indications of more serious damage to the first vessel than had been imagined.

Following this, two further attacks were launched on the much-punished submarine. One of these came from a Catalina flying boat which, although able to drop its depth charges while the front gunner pumped about one hundred rounds at the conning tower, was itself hit and forced to turn for home.

But the flying boat had not arrived alone; with it had been a Wellington from Gibraltar, 'R for Roger'. Coming down to only 80 ft, the captain brought his machine in for a low steady approach so that the depth charges could inflict the final blow to the sub. Then, just as the charges were about to be released, the Nazi gunners, who had up to now held their fire against the fresh assailant, let fly with everything they had. 'R for Roger' was suddenly flying into a seemingly solid wall of hot metal. Almost at the same moment that the depth charges were dropped, the crew of the Wellington felt a severe jolt as the port wing took the full weight of the Germans' punishment. In a moment, the big aircraft went out of control and, at such a low altitude, the end was inevitable: the machine crashed into the sea to the accompaniment of a ragged cheer from the Nazis.

There was only one survivor from 'R for Robert'. Unconscious, but tossed out on impact, the pilot came to as the salt water splashed over his face, and his fogged brain was just able to register that about 15 yd away floated the dinghy that had automatically inflated as the Wellington had crashed. Scarcely aware of what he was doing, the captain struck out for the little rubber boat that was his only hope of sanctuary. Groggily, he took the side rope in his almost numb fingers and, with a final, supreme effort, hauled himself into the boat and then slumped as though dead.

Three or four minutes later, the pilot was brought to his senses as the dinghy was rammed. The submarine crew were seemingly convinced that the man in the boat was dead and had barged into the dinghy as they escaped from the scene. Realizing that he had been taken for dead, the airman stayed motionless within full view of six Nazi sailors who were going about their duties in the conning tower. His ploy succeeded and the vessel, still on the surface, made off in a westerly direction leaving the lonely occupant of the dinghy to await rescue. This arrived at 09:10 hrs on 9 January when HMS *Active* picked him up and treated his facial wounds before taking him to Gibraltar.

Meanwhile, Wellington 'N for Nuts', was still in the area. It observed a large burst of flame—possibly the damaged Catalina—about three miles from the U-boat before the latter made off and, at 23:03 hrs, the bomber left the area temporarily, to attempt to make contact with destroyers some distance away. This duty completed, it returned to the scene of the action only to find that the submarine had vanished.

This news was received in La Senia, and another Wellington was sent off shortly afterwards with orders to carry out a square search and drop marine markers. In company with a pair of rocket-armed Hudsons, six destroyers reported that they were hunting in the area at 01:00 hrs on the 9th and, one hour later, two more Wellingtons took off to continue what was the largest 'Operation Swamp' sortie to date.

Meanwhile, the second part of the operation—the Alicante hunt—was developing a character all its own. It had started at dawn on 8 January and had been rewarded by a sighting at 07:51 hrs when Wellington 'N for Nuts' had found a partially-submerged U-boat with only its conning tower visible. Realizing that they had come upon a submarine in the act of diving, the pilot of the Wellington immediately put down the nose of his machine and, making a steep diving turn, released a depth charge at 100 ft. Five more followed, straddling the target, and an oil patch, some 70 yd in diameter, soon appeared. Two more depth charges were dropped ahead of the slick, but, as these seemed to have had no effect, a smoke marker was sent down before 'N for Nuts' went off to search a wider area for the next couple of hours.

Seventeen minutes after 'N for Nuts' had made its attack, a second Wellington appeared on the scene: 'Z for Zebra' of the same squadron flying at 2,000 ft. This machine had only just arrived when its crew caught sight of a submarine at much the same latitude, only three miles distant and with its decks awash. Immediately, the pilot dived the machine to 200 ft, but on this occasion the Nazi crew were too quick for the airmen. By the time the aircraft was in position, the enemy had vanished, although the submarine was reported to be still in the area by the crew of a Catalina so, at 16:00 hrs, destroyers were called in to continue the surface hunt.

If the RAF had anything to do with it, this one was not going to get away. Two more Wellingtons were despatched from Gibraltar at 10:08 hrs, setting course for 'N for Nuts' and 'Z for Zebra's' sighting positions at 10:08 hrs, and another two were sent in to widen the hunt before midday. Time passed, but no further reports of U-boats were received, so it was decided to add a further five Wellingtons to the force in the evening and, by the middle of the night of 9–10 January, a total of seventeen Wellingtons and twelve Hudsons were engaged in the extended hunt.

At last, the long-awaited signal came in from a destroyer, HMS *Atherstone*, at 01:00 hrs. She reported that she had dropped a 'considerable number' of depth charges near to the most northeasterly limit of the hunting area after making a strong Asdic contact. This was followed by a fine example of co-operation between air and naval forces. The report zone was being patrolled by a clutch of Wellingtons, and it was one of these, 'L for London', that reported a fresh contact one hour and forty minutes later. It seemed from the position that this was not the same U-boat that had attracted the attention of the destroyer, yet all U-boats were grist to the mill, so the aircraft's information was passed to two other surface vessels, as well as to base. However, such is the nature of war and sea searches in general that, following the disappearance of the contacts, it was decided to abandon the southerly searches around Cape de Gata and to concentrate instead on the vicinity of Ibiza, with effect from 14:30 hrs.

Only one Wellington was at first involved in this new hunt, supported by three Hudsons and a Martin Marauder between 15:00 and 16:00 hrs. Then the hunt area was again widened, both north and south of the Mediterranean island, until dawn on 11 January.

With the trail growing cold it was left to a Wellington—the type which had been the mainstay of the RAF's contribution—to make the final report. This came from 'K for King' at 17:06 hrs on Monday 10 January. At first the sea seemed to be featureless, but then one of the crew gave a start and rubbed his weary eyes. He was almost sure that he had seen something to break the monotony of the waste of water below. Yes, there it was; there was no mistaking the tiny tell-tale plume of water about eight miles away. The airman's yell of recognition immediately brought his colleagues once again to full alertness. There was no mistake: as the Wellington lost height and came to within three miles of the target it was clear that the wake was made by a conning tower. Then, just as the Wellington banked to take up its attack position, the final swirl of water died away and, in a last-minute dive, the U-boat escaped.

For the next four and a half hours, 'K for King' patiently searched the area until 20:08, when it radioed the position of the suspect to two destroyers which appeared over the horizon. Three more Wellingtons were diverted to the area and then, on the morning of 11 January, the hunt was restricted to the north of the island where the last sighting had taken place. Despite a concentrated search, which had involved no fewer than eighteen Wellingtons during the night, it seemed as though the submarine must have got away.

With first light new plans were announced: if nothing was discovered during the day, three aircraft would be allocated that evening to hunting along the estimated track of the submarine from the last known position. These aircraft had to fly at low altitude with the ASV switched off whenever the moon permitted a visual search. In the event the trio drew a blank and as a result the greatest hunt of 'Operation Swamp' was called off, with the last aircraft returning to base at 10:15 hrs on 12 January.

Faced with this lack of positive results, it would be only too easy to judge the operation as a failure—indeed this opinion was freely stated not long afterwards—but official sources disagreed strongly with this view. Certainly, 'Swamp' had made heavy demands on a variety of manpower sources, but it had been successful as a deterrent in areas which were known to be frequented by U-boats. Despite aircraft losses, there had been nine aerial assaults against submarines, the majority of these being made by Wellingtons engaged in the tedious operation of sea search.

Night patrol techniques had certainly come a long way since those first Leigh Light Wellingtons. The original, crude operating method, where a lamp was raised and lowered with block and tackle, had been refined to the final hydraulic operation, although even then the 'light man's' controls were in the front turret position and a loose gun was fired over his head! Altogether, the sea Wimpy had a fair measure of success against U-boats at night, despite the fact that the stick of eight, 250-lb depth charges had to be released from a hair-raising altitude of about 50 ft to ensure that the casings did not break up on impact. In their 'webbed-foot' role, Wellingtons even gained some affectionate nicknames: those with 'stickle-back' aerials were known as 'Goofingtons' while the ones equipped with eighteen-inch torpedoes were 'Fishingtons'.

Chapter 6
Striking force

The tide of war had brought a very different atmosphere to air operations by August 1940, heralded by Wellingtons being set to attack the vaguely-described 'targets of opportunity' as troops were being lifted from the beaches of northern France, and especially Dunkirk. By now, Great Britain herself was fighting for survival, and the outcome of the Battle of Britain would decide whether the Nazis would invade England's very shores. Every household in the land would be issued with a leaflet bearing the heading 'What to do if the Invader Comes', and giving the sound advice to 'sit tight'—a lesson learned the hard way from experience in France where the hordes of refugees had hampered military operations. Yet, despite the gravity of the situation, the policy was still to strike back at the enemy whenever possible, and the night of 2 August was to prove one of the most significant in the war to date.

Twenty-four hours before, both the heart and the crowded East End of London had been bombed in 'one of the miscalculations of history', as a military correspondent was to describe it. Great Britain was stung into ordering a reprisal attack against the German capital of Berlin, and a force of eighty-one bombers was duly despatched; the largest that had ever been assembled. Instructions to the raiders were strict—if specific targets could not be identified, the bombers' loads were to be brought home again.

The mainstay of the attacking force were Vickers Wellingtons, of which No 149 Squadron from Mildenhall provided eight. The first trio climbed into the summer evening sky at 20:50 hrs: Sgt Harrison's *P9248* 'D', P/O Peterson's *R3164* 'B' and Sqn Ldr Kerr's *P9268* 'H'. Four minutes later F/O Burton's *R6163* 'G' and P/O Panter's *T2459* 'J' followed. These were joined after another four minutes by *L7812* 'R for Robert', commanded by Flt

Lt Griffith-Jones, and *R3206* 'M for Monkey', with darkened roundels like the rest of the formation and an unusual dope scheme designed to make the aircraft less visible in the probing searchlight beams. The captain of 'M for Monkey' was the same P/O Michael Sherwood who had been involved in the abortive 'blue light' experiments, flying with a new crew consisting of P/O Osborn as second pilot, and four Sergeants: Wood, the observer, Digby in charge of the radio, and Laird and Dwyer in the nose and tail turrets. Last away at exactly 21:00 hrs was P/O Green's *R3212* 'T'.

Despite the anticipation and apprehension of the aircrews, the attack was to prove something of an anti-climax. Searchlights swept the sky, it is true, and anti-aircraft fire was encountered too, but the main characteristic of the mission was the need for sustained concentration: for example, 'M for Monkey' was in the air for a total of seven hours and twenty-five minutes, three hours of which was flying 'blind' on instruments alone. However, it was generally agreed that the attack had been a success. In the words of the Squadron log, it had accomplished the intention 'to attack industrial targets and aerodromes, and cause maximum amount of disturbance— mission carried out safely—all aircraft returned to base.'

Last home had been Michael Sherwood and P/O Green. The sense of relief which followed is perhaps summed up best in the words of the former who recalls 'After de-briefing, breakfast in the Mess always tasted very good. Then a bath and bed, and perhaps listening on one's own radio to any other Wellingtons speaking to base, and calculating [on other occasions] who had and who had not returned.'

* * *

There was no such 'happy landing' as this for P/O Kenneth Wallis after a mission with No 104 Squadron's Wellingtons flying a sortie from Elsham Wolds on the night of 21–22 September 1941. Kenneth had previously been a Lysander pilot, but now, at the controls of the big Vickers bomber *L7886* 'X for X-ray', he had set course for the primary target at Frankfurt. The city had been obscured by cloud so that there had been no alternative but to carry the load of bombs back to the coast and drop it on the secondary objective before setting course for home.

Naturally, the extended route to the alternative target had taken its toll of the Wellington's fuel, but there seemed plenty to power the machine home when the British coast came into view—plenty, that is, unless there were any more problems.

The fact that more problems did arise was only another set-back in what had proved to be 'one of those days'. The welcoming coast of home could hardly be made out as the whole of southern England lay in a great blanket of fog through which nothing could be identified, let alone home base. (Remember, these were the days before the introduction of FIDO for fog dispersal.) The Pilot Officer's first reaction was the obvious one—to fly north and seek a landing ground free from the enveloping blanket. However the flickering needles on the petrol gauges warned P/O Wallis that he had better come up with another idea...and fast!

Nothing daunted, Ken turned to his 'Darkie' emergency radio, and received an acknowledgement from RAF Binbrook as he followed the pathway that British searchlights marked out to assist homeward-bound bombers. These welcome beams could be picked out under the covering of fog as diffuse pools of light in the curtain of gloom. Taking his eyes away from them for a moment, the pilot's eyes strayed in the disciplined way of a competent pilot over the dials in front of him. At first glance all seemed to be in order, but then he blinked and took a second look at the all-important petrol gauges. There was no doubt about it...the worst had happened...the fuel tanks had run dry. For a moment he could not believe it, because the twin engines were turning over sweetly enough, but then this could be explained by the discrepancy between the registered quantity of fuel and what really remained. 'Perhaps the instruments aren't accurate', Wallis muttered to himself. Clinging to this hope that he knew in his heart was groundless, he promptly contacted the Binbrook station and requested that the Chance Light—the tall mobile beacon which resembled a miniature lighthouse—be switched on and off so that he might note his position before making the first attempt to put the Wellington down safely.

Kenneth's first try at landing was a failure and the nine attempts that followed, using timed circuits, were similarly unsuccessful. With motors still purring sweetly, he put the bomber into a gentle climb and again called up Binbrook over the radio, while at the back of his mind ran the thought that the fuel gauges must be inaccurate after all.

Wallis asked Binbrook for permission to order his crew to bale out before making any further attempts to land, only to receive the astonishing reply that he was to fly to Linton-on-Ouse and land there. Reacting swiftly to this absurd order, Ken repeated that the tower had already been informed that the instruments indicated no fuel. As if to underline Ken's protest, the engines chose this moment to cut out. Moments later, they coughed into life again as the final dregs of petrol reached them, screamed in fine pitch, and then gave up the ghost. Further discussion was pointless, so Binbrook tower was firmly told that all aboard the Wellington were about to bale out.

As the crew started to jump, the young Pilot Officer was fastening on his own parachute. This proved to be no easy task for he could not find the release handle under the cushion that formed part of the equipment, and he had to unfasten everything, extract the handle and then re-attach the main hooks, all the while keeping an eye on the behaviour of 'X for X-ray'. It had now fallen into a glide punctuated with occasional bursts of power from the engines. Wallis had not switched these off, for even a small gain in height might be vital in the new situation.

The altimeter was showing just 700 ft when Ken took his last look down the length of the now-deserted bomber. The great lattice tube could be seen in every detail and was etched sharply on the young man's mind, the more so due to the fact that an interior light still burned, throwing up the details in sharp focus. Then, stepping down from the high, port-side seat, Ken opened the front hatch and prepared to drop through.

In the second before he let himself tumble from the aircraft, the Pilot Officer was aware that something felt very wrong: his movements were easy and unhampered, far too easy for those of a man wearing a parachute and harness. Something made him take a second glance at the inside of his stricken machine. As he looked back, he mentally blessed the thoughtful colleague who had left the light on, for without this he would have not been able to see that the precious parachute was still serving as a cushion in his pilot's seat! He was, in fact, connected to the parachute by the webbing straps of the harness that had become detached as he groped for the elusive release handle earlier! Had he jumped—and he had been only a split second away from doing so—he would have ended up trailing and helpless, attached to the doomed Wellington!

While the altimeter needle slowly but surely revolved round the dial, the pilot moved with swift decision. A lunge and a grab towards the seat secured the pack and, gathering up the tangle of straps that had so nearly been the cause of his death, he took the whole bundle in his arms, crouched poised over the open hatch for a fraction of a second, and then dropped his head and toppled into the night.

He had no sensation of falling, and it was not too difficult for Ken to keep his mind firmly under control. Once free from the aircraft, he released the bundle from his clasped arms and, a matter of seconds later, pulled the rip-cord that would release his canopy. It always seems to take an inordinate length of time for a parachute to open, and

Ken had split seconds now in which to wonder with amazing calm and detachment whether all the turmoil of webbing would sort itself out. The answer came with a painful jerk accompanied by a sharp report like that of a pistol, announcing that the great canopy had deployed. In the same moment, he heard a new sound, familiar and at the same time out of place: that of the wind sighing over the airframe of his doomed bomber which, making great circles as it plunged to its own destruction, was now making straight for him. He hung in the air, impotently, unable to do much to avoid the aircraft in the blackness of the unfriendly September night.

It was almost on him now, its great black bulk showing up clearly against the softer darkness of the sky. Then, as if guided by an unseen pilot, the Wellington that had a few moments before seemed bent on slaying its one-time pilot, now lifted a wing when only a matter of yards away and changed course. A few moments later it crashed to its inevitable end seeming to burst into a thousand pieces in open country at Holton-le-Moor.

Ken was so fascinated by the drama that had unfolded beneath his feet, that he did not notice the earth coming up to meet him and the jolt as he himself hit the ground was that much sharper. It was no text-book landing. As he rolled over, his senses dulled by concussion, Ken was aware that the shock of the impact had done his back no good. However, the pain was mercifully blacked out almost before he could feel it as he lapsed into total unconsciousness.

It was about thirty minutes later that comprehension came gradually flowing back. At first it returned slowly so that he wondered with an air of detachment why he was flying in a field, and then, as he became more fully aware, he noticed small details such as the droplets of fog as they dripped from the twigs of a nearby hedge. He lay for a moment and gathered his thoughts. Clearly he must make a move and it did not seem as though he was too badly hurt to walk. The only problem was that he had no idea where he was and therefore which direction he should go. Then a sudden thought struck him as his mind became clearer. He always carried a World War 1 type Mauser pistol inside his flying suit and, drawing it out, he fired two shots into the air to attract attention. After a brief pause, they were answered by a shout from the men who were searching the countryside not far off, and it was not long before a Home Guard and the local policeman were crossing the field towards him. The remainder of the crew of 'X for X-ray' had all landed without injury along the Caistor–Market Rasen road and had entered the record books by being the first men from 103 Squadron to parachute to safety over Great Britain. P/O

Kenneth Wallis was sufficiently recovered to return to operations by 10 October. Happily, he survived the war and became the well-known gyrocopter pioneer: Wng Cdr K.H. Wallis, CEng, FRAeS, FRSA, RAF (Retd).

* * *

If most moments remembered by the men who flew Wellingtons were full of action and stress, there were still times, even in the heat of action, when humour relieved the tension.

One such that is recalled by the pilot of a Wellington Ic took place during an October night attack on the power station at Weissling. Takeoff had been at 17:40 hrs, and the bombers found the night unusually dark, even for the time of year. The trip to the target area had been uneventful, but problems arose when it came to identifying the power station because of the lack of illumination. The bomber swept round in circles attempting to pick out the Weissling station but, although the navigator, Sgt Williams, had brought the machine and its crew of six accurately to the vicinity, it looked as though *R3284* would have to be diverted to the secondary target.

The captain knew that their presence was noted by the enemy below, so there seemed no reason to exercise undue caution. Consequently, he decided to order his second aft to launch a flare so that the crew could identify the power station once and for all.

Now, in those days, flares were dropped from a Wellington by the simple expedient of merely lobbing them down a chute near to the rear of the aircraft. The second pilot duly moved into position and prepared for the launch by picking up the relevant dogged rod. This rod was shaped much like the starting crank used on older-style cars, and was necessary because the chute first had to be extended so that it protruded far enough outside the aircraft to ensure that the flare was cast clear of the tailplane. So, the second pilot (whose name is known but would prefer to remain anonymous!) set to work with the rod while, confident that their problems of identification were now just about over, the bomb aimer lay at his switches and prepared to loose the load of 25 BCs (incendiaries) and three 500-lb high-explosive bombs (NDTs).

The six aboard were tensely silent as they waited for the welcome 'Bombs gone' announcement over the intercom after which they could head for home. Nothing happened...no flare of light...no bombs. Instead the headphones crackled as the second Dickie broke in with a message for his superior. 'I say, Captain, I've just dropped the rod down the flare chute...hope it doesn't hurt anyone!'

* * *

Four days previously, a Wellington of the Ia variety, *P2917*, had departed from No 37 Squadron's base at Feltwell with Sgt Smith acting as navigator and P/O (Nobby) Clarke at the controls. It had left at 21:05 hrs to make a night attack on a petroleum storage installation in Frankfurt. The target had not proved difficult to identify and the enemy opposition had been no more troublesome than the briefing had led the crews to expect, although it had certainly been determined. So, with bombs dropped, *P2917* was soon well into the return journey and flying above the North Sea. It was at this stage that the sortie made its claim to be remembered as a 'shaky do'.

The first indication that all was not well came in the starboard engine readings on the instruments in front of the pilot. It did not take much detective work to find out what was wrong: all on board who had a view of that side could see quite plainly that the engine was well alight and blazing fiercely. In cases such as this, the fire extinguishers in the engine bay could usually be relied upon to douse the flames. In this particular instance, however, success was only partial...and worse was to come. Unaware that the captain was calling on all his skill to maintain control of a Wellington which was suddenly behaving 'differently', one of the crew watched, open-mouthed, as the airscrew from the offending engine suddenly came loose and vanished, a spinning, silver disc, into the void below. Despite this 'slight hitch', the ability of the Wellington to fly on one engine, allied to the skill of the pilot, meant that the aircraft reached dry land safely. P/O 'Nobby' Clarke, captain of *P2918*, was eventually to be awarded a well-deserved Distinguished Flying Cross.

* * *

If the cream of the recollections of the Wellington crews consists largely of the earlier bombing attacks of the Second World War, this is chiefly due to the fact that this was the time when the type formed the backbone of the RAF's attacking arm. The four-engined types had yet to enter service, and the long-held belief in a bomber force capable of striking at an enemy day and night without additional protection lingered on. There was also the somewhat naive belief that using long-distance machines to drop propaganda material on the population of Nazi Germany would have a more signal result, hopefully, than that achieved by bombing missions.

Thus it was that four Wellingtons, *L7770* commanded by Sqn Ldr Griffiths, *L4225* by Flt Sgt Brent, *R2701* by Flt Sgt Downey, and *L4309* under Sgt Hemsley, were ordered to be prepared for a 'Nickel' sortie, dropping leaflets, and the four were flown to Newmarket from Upper Heyford for the operational crews to take over. But before this the machines had to be flown to Mildenhall for the 'Operations and Intelligence Officers to interview the crews and inform them of any recent information'—a process yet to be summed up as 'briefing'.

Just before they were due to leave Mildenhall, Griffiths' *L7770* was found to have developed leaks in the oxygen equipment. As there was not enough time to get hold of a replacement Wellington, it was decided that the operation would be carried out by the three other machines on their own, dropping the leaflets over Hanover before making a reconnaissance of Bremen and Wilhelmshaven.

First away at 23:02 hrs was Flt Sgt Brent's *L4225*. The Wimpy set off in thick haze but, scarcely had the machine become airborne, before the pilot realized that the aileron control was not functioning correctly. A little investigation revealed that this was caused by a bent connecting rod running between the control column and that of the dual control position. Despite this, the second set-back of the sortie, it was decided to carry on to the target area. Only some thirty minutes had passed when the pilot started to find the aircraft even harder to control and, suspecting that something else was wrong he sent one of the crew aft to look for the source of the problem. It was obvious that the trouble was due to something more serious than just a bent connecting rod.

It was the work of a moment to discover the reason. No mechanical problem this: the cause for the pilot's difficulties was the method of stacking the weight of paper that formed the load of 'bumph'. In the manner usually adopted by the Squadron, the leaflets had been piled up on the rest bunk, and the upper ones on several piles had slipped, probably during the initial climb. They had now fallen down and were partially jamming the control crank. In fact, they were lodged so firmly that there was no hope of dislodging them in the air and it was decided to return to base. Despite low visibility at Mildenhall, *L4225* did manage to land, one and a quarter hours after take-off. As the Wellington touched down, the pilot's lack of control took its toll; the rear portion of the fuselage was damaged.

Meanwhile, there were no such problems for Flt Sgt Brent's colleagues in Hemsley's *L4309*, which took off three minutes after *L4225*. The pilot set course for a point 15 miles north of Emden, climbing to 18,000 ft, and, as had been pre-arranged, the navigation lights were switched off ten minutes after crossing the British coast. Then, when the Wellington was some 20 miles east of Borkum, course was set for the target at Hanover, and at exactly 02:20 hrs 300,000 pamphlets were unloaded over that city.

Two minutes later the silence on the Wellington's intercom system was broken by the voice of the rear gunner, Sgt Simpson. 'Enemy fighter to starboard, and behind!' he warned, adding 'Passing across behind us!' Alerted now, the other members of the crew waited for the seemingly inevitable attack. None came. Simpson, unable to bring his guns to bear on the fast machine, just had time to note that it looked like a Messerschmitt 109 before it flashed across the wake of the Wellingon some 30 yd behind. Incredibly, the German must have missed seeing the enemy, for he did not return to attack, and the bomber was able to set course for Bremen.

Once over the city, Sgt Hemsley's crew found the area covered by haze which extended up to 16,000 ft so that the ground was practically invisible. This haze may well have saved the RAF men since the searchlights were very active and were working in conjunction with single-engined fighters, two of which were observed well astern.

Realizing that they could do little more, the captain now turned for home over Wilhelmshaven, setting course for Great Yarmouth. Navigation was proving a problem, partly because there were no direction-finding facilities, and also because the westerly wind was much stronger than had been predicted by the meteorological report. Several changes of course had to be made until a fix was finally obtained when the machine was at 3,500 ft over Amsterdam. By now fuel was running low, so they headed for Manston 'on receipt of W/T instructions' (their own base was fogbound), and a landing was made here at 07:15 hrs with only forty gallons of fuel remaining in the tanks. 'No A/A fire was observed', concluded Sgt Hemsley's report.

The thick mist that had prevented *L4309*'s return to base had been lingering for a long time. In fact, it had been hanging over the airfield when the third Wellington, *L2701* with Flt Sgt Downey in command, took off on the previous evening at 23:10 hrs. His was to prove an uneventful sortie, much of it carried out at an altitude of 18,000 ft. The first course was set for a point similar to that adopted by Hemsley, then the pilot turned for Hanover. After the leaflets had been dropped, Downey was able to cruise over the city for a full half-hour, seemingly unobserved, before making for the point where they had first crossed the German coast. They later saw some lights below and assumed that these indicated a built-up area in Holland. Subsequently, F/O Challins had trouble finding land and they flew around for some time before 'Dungeness was finally located'. The final landfall was made at Manston at 06:30 hrs.

None of the men in the crews of these Wellingtons were to survive the war. The same applied to those aboard the ill-starred machine that was grounded at Mildenhall, with the single exception of Sqn Ldr Griffiths' rear gunner, Cpl Bickerstaffe, who became a Flight Sergeant and was last heard of living in Nottingham.

Bickerstaff was an experienced NCO, and was to be awarded a Distinguished Flying Medal after an action only five days later. This was a daylight operation over the Nazi naval base at Heligoland involving twelve Wellingtons, with the Corporal acting as rear gunner in *N2958*, of which J.E. Griffiths—now described as an Acting Wing Commander—was the pilot. These were the only two from the crew of *L7770* which had been forced to withdraw from the earlier night mission.

The twelve machines making up this new attacking force had taken off at around 11:43 hrs and, after climbing to a height of 1,000 ft, had passed over Yarmouth under ten-tenths cloud and above the thick haze that reduced visibility to only two miles. Indeed the weather was such that Griffiths decided to make for a point off Terschilling in order to obtain an accurate fix before setting course for the target area. however, the weather deteriorated steadily so that, by the time the bombers had crossed the North Sea and the coast of Holland could be made out, it was 13:05 hrs and the aircraft were at only 600 ft, flying in fine rain. They were heading towards Heligoland, hoping to deceive the enemy flak vessels into thinking that this was the intended objective.

Soon the weather became even worse and the formation was forced down to only 300 ft. Forty-two minutes later, when course was altered for Schillig Roads, visibility was only half a mile, and they had to descend to 200 ft in the worsening weather conditions. Nevertheless the Wellingtons managed to keep formation. The only sign of life below was five trawlers with their nets out which fired four red-ball signal cartridges. Then a submarine was sighted a few minutes later, dead ahead and riding on the surface. When this vessel fired similar lights to those sent up by the trawlers, the formation leader replied with a rapid pair of red-ball signals on the off-chance that this might be the recognition sign, although in this he was obviously mistaken, since the submarine immediately crash-dived!

About ten minutes now passed before a battle cruiser and cruiser were spotted steaming south at about 10 knots, and the Wellington formation swung round to avoid passing above these

Above *R1459* at Elsham Wold in October 1941 after hitting a barrage balloon cable (W/C K. H. Wallis).

Below The pilot's log book and a photograph recalling the balloon cable incident of *PM-X* (W/C K. H. Wallis).

Above A 75 Squadron Wellington after a raid on Berlin in April 1941. Left to right: Flt Sgt D. Sharp, Flt Lt C. Hill, Sgt P. Parrott, F/O Thompson, Sgt Chambers and, just out of shot, Sgt W. Elliot (Denis Sharp).

Left At work on the port engine of a Wellington at Waterbeach in March 1941 (from Norman Didwell).

Above right A source of spares — a cannibalized Wellington with the outer wing panels already taken (Bruce Robertson collection).

Right The first 4,000-lb bomb is unloaded in Burma (from Norman Didwell).

Left *HD975* shows the nose turret removed to reduce weight (T. H. Claridge).

Middle left A Mk Ic, *HD975* 'L', with Africans in attendance (T. H. Claridge).

Bottom left The 'Youngers Beer' Wellington. Note that the nose turret is sealed, as are the gun slits (Imperial War Museum).

Right 'T for Tommy' of 466 Squadron with armourers and a flight mechanic electrician. The badge was red and yellow (H. E. Dickson).

Below The crew of Wellington Mk X *MF560*. Left to right: Sgt Field, Sgt Judd, Flt Sgt Fleming, Sgt Wiseman, Sgt Brown, (front) Sgt Loxton (J. Brown).

Above T10 *PG267* of No 5 ANS seen in June 1952. Note the individual letter on the nose (P. Farnell).

Below Inside a T10, showing the navigator's seat aft of the main spar and the radar set on the left (P. Farnell).

Above Refuelling a Wellington T10 from a bowser at No 5 ANS in 1952 (P. Farnell).

Below The instrument panel and controls of a Wellington T10. The compass is clearly visible in the bottom centre (P. Farnell).

Above The last Wellington to survive intact, T10 *MF628* is normally in the RAF Museum but is seen here at Abingdon in 1968 (L. J. Dickson).

Below *K4094*, the Vickers B.9/32 and virtual prototype of the Wellington (Chaz Bowyer collection).

warships, at the same time keeping an eye on eight cargo boats also proceeding south. These also shot off four red-ball cartridges before suddenly opening fire. Then three destroyers appeared from nowhere and joined in the party.

The Wellington formation, flying at no more than 200 ft, presented a juicy target to the naval gunners below. The two warships that had been spotted earlier now joined in with uncomfortable accuracy and the bombers could feel the force of the exploding shells outside, rocking and bumping the aircraft. The RAF men wisely decided to keep their distance!

'Fighters!' There was only time for the single word of warning before the first of the interceptors came in close with guns blazing, followed by two others. The time was exactly 14:36. The cry from a gunner of the first aircraft of the bombers' No 1 Section had been echoed throughout the formation, so the three Messerschmitt 109s that had opened the attack from the direction of Wangerooge were greeted with combined fire from all of the Wellingtons. Cpl A. Bickerstaffe made his own contribution from the tail of the leader's machine where Acting Wing Cdr Griffiths sat beside the pilot, Sqn Ldr McKee.

In the brief pause that followed, there was time to take stock of the situation. It was abundantly clear that the atrocious weather on its own would make it impossible to deliver the three 500-lb bombs that each Wellington carried on the Nazi warships in Schillig Roads. So far, there had been only one casualty—Sgt Brace's *N2986*—which had been seen going down in flames from No 4 Section before the single-seaters had attacked; evidently a victim of the wickedly accurate fire from the ships.

The pause for reflection was lamentably brief. Three fresh 109s had appeared from the cover of the mist and closed in on the now-depleted No 4 Section, diving from astern and slightly above to carry out one attack each before breaking away. Two minutes later, the single-seaters were augmented by the appearance of a trio of twin-engined Messerschmitt 110s on the port beam which seemed to concentrate on McKee's Wimpy. They closed in from below, taking careful aim, and large amounts of white tracer passed within two feet of their intended victim's fuselage before they, or another three 110s, turned on No 4 Section at the rear and made single attacks in the manner of the earlier 109s.

It was ten minutes before the next assault came from the twin-engined defenders, which again concentrated their attention on the rear Section, while almost simultaneously three more began to harry Sections 1 and 2. The enemy aircraft had hardly broken off their attack when the Wellington crews saw a heartening spectacle: one of the Messerschmitt 110s suddenly dived vertically towards the water with its port wing a mass of flames.

Another appeared only minutes later, thirsting for revenge, and latching on to the lead Wellington, flying about 20 ft behind and 50 ft above. Presented with such an inviting target, Cpl Bickerstaffe in the tail turret took careful but speedy aim and fired a long burst at the Nazi. The Messerschmitt seemed to hover momentarily as the Englishman's fire passed directly through the attacker's cockpit. Then with a great burst of flame, the wing inboard of the port engine was swallowed up and the inferno spread rapidly to the rest of the aircraft. Inevitably, the fighter fell into a vertical dive that ended as it struck the water in a sheet of flame.

At almost the same moment, another twin-engined aircraft was seen going down, partly hidden by No 3 Section, and closely followed by yet another 110. Four separate fires, coming from twin-engined types, were sending up columns of black and oily smoke from the water. Seconds later it was noticed that both of the No 3 aircraft of Nos 1 and 2 Sections had vanished, as had the third Wellington from No 3 (No 2, Brace's *N2986*, had been accounted for earlier). Notes added to the official report later agree that the third Wellington from this Section was one of those sent down at the height of the engagement—F/O Cooper's bomber. Some claimed they had seen the Wimpy heading for the German coast with the undercarriage down.

The missing pair from the two first sections had met an untimely end when P/O Lewis' *N2870* had been made uncontrollable by the naval guns and had collided with Flt Sgt Downey's Wellington (*N2991*); they had gone down together. Seconds later, Griffiths, in the machine which was being so well defended aft by Bickerstaffe, noticed a new gap in the punished British formation. This had been left by Flt Sgt Healey's machine (*N2886*), which became the victim of a sudden burst of continuous anti-aircraft fire from the ships below when the fighters temporarily withdrew. It was proving impossible to keep clear of the enemy vessels in the poor visibility and the Wellingtons had inadvertently flown directly above them and into a fiery mass of bursting shells.

The fight had lasted for almost half an hour when the Messerschmitts came in for their final assault. The 110s, easily identified by their twin engines and double tails, streamed down from behind and, although their fire was returned, neither side gained an advantage. The six surviving Wellingtons set course disconsolately for Yarmouth. Although a single Luftwaffe machine was noticed on the port beam about ten minutes later, its pilot made no attempt to attack, and the six reached their base at Newmarket without further incident.

But there was a further tragedy in store. All the returning Wellingtons had brought their bombs home except for one, commanded by Flt Lt Hetherington who had dumped what had appeared to be his entire load in the sea. Five of the battered formation made good landings, but Hetherington was evidently having difficulties. For some reason the bomb doors were hanging open, the approach was faulty and *N2957*, with its New Zealand pilot, piled up in a field beyond the boundary of the airfield. The time was exactly 17:30 hrs when Hetherington died, along with his radio operator 'Pete' Entwhistle and nose gunner 'Jock' Sharp. The fact that not all the bombs had been dumped was revealed by Sgt Louis Parton, the tail gunner. He added in his own handwriting above his signature on the official form: 'One bomb hung up. I know as I got the badly injured Observer out.' Testimony to a quiet act of heroism.

Chapter 7
From eagles to doves

The Vickers Wellington was conceived, designed and first constructed in 1936, by which time it was becoming apparent that re-arming to keep pace with Nazi Germany could no longer be delayed. In truth, the bomber could fairly claim to be the backbone of Bomber Command until the appearance of its new four-engined aircraft. The Wellington's primary function was therefore that for which it had been designed—taking war into the enemy's territory. This strategy had been tentatively implemented twenty or so years previously with the arrival of specialist aircraft when the First World War ended.

Yet the Wellington was sufficiently adaptable to be pressed into other roles during its long history. Even as late as June 1944, a Mk XIV, individually identified as 'G for George' and serialized *HF336*, flew from Ford in Sussex for the purpose of experimental night photography.

But there were other duties which the Vickers Wellington performed that called for no special modifications, merely a temporary change of use. One which is now largely forgotten is the work of the Famine Relief Flight over Aden which pre-dated the well-known but similar 'Operation Manna' after the end of the war in Europe.

The story of the Famine Relief Flight really began in 1941. That was the year when the last rain had fallen in Hadramaut, the part of the then Protectorate of Aden which lay inland from the coast of the Gulf of Aden. The whole territory had an area of 42,000 square miles that had to support 100,000 inhabitants.

Two consecutive waterless years followed the rain of 1941, and to this was added an extra, man-made tragedy. For, although there was no armed conflict in Hadramaut itself, war was even so affecting the lives of its inhabitants since many of them existed on incomes derived from whole or part ownership of Far East properties, chiefly in Java and Malaya. The Japanese occupation of these areas had therefore deprived the inhabitants of a combined income totalling £6,000,000. As a consequence of these combined disasters, famine now haunted this part of the Aden Protectorate.

By the beginning of 1944, the sight of virtually naked children, standing beside the main roads among the bones of dead camels, was becoming increasingly commonplace. Although they were still capable of standing the children were so thin that their shaven heads appeared too large for the rest of their frame, while their faces, dominated by sunken, haggard eyes, seemed to be those of old men and women. That they now stood at the roadsides was due to a last desperate strategem of their parents who hoped against hope that a convoy returning empty to the coast at Mukalla might realize that they had been deliberately abandoned, pick them up and carry them away from the interior where conditions were at their worst. Just how desperate the measure was, may be judged from the fact that the lack of any kind of fodder had greatly reduced the camel population; the number of transport animals had been reduced by two thirds. It was to remedy this tragic state of affairs that the British government ordered prompt action to be taken and voted £300,000 for relief work.

As a preliminary, the Governor of the Aden Protectorate carried out an inspection of the Hadramaut, and took the only course open to him in the available time—he flew into the interior. Relief measures called for the movement of vast quantities of food, milk and medical supplies to the inland centres where soup kitchens were to be set up and free supplies distributed. At the same time, emergency hospitals were established, staffed by volunteers from Aden, and buildings were turned into crèches/schools where hundreds of children, some of them orphans, could be cared for. It was clear from these plans that the only way of implementing them as quickly as possible was to use air transport, so the RAF was called in.

In the meantime, the first part of the operation had already begun with hundreds of bags of millet and maize being sent to the port at Mukalla along the Gulf coast from Aden. The task facing the RAF was to distribute the provisions to the inland areas.

On Tuesday 25 April 1944 the members of the Famine Relief Flight which had been formed three days before at HQ, RAF Middle East were moved to Aden; and on 27 April they were again moved, this time to Riyan. So far the Flight had no aircraft, but that is not to say that time was being wasted, for at the same time No 168 Maintenance Unit was busy modifying six new Wellington Xs that had arrived from the United Kingdom, fitting them mainly for supply dropping. As the individual Wellingtons were completed they were forwarded to Riyan, the last arriving on 7 May.

As might be expected, the personnel of the Flight were drawn from a variety of sources, the Army included, with the Wellington crews being found from the Middle East Training School for Parachutists at Ramat Divid. These included five parachute instructors who were picked to supervise the supply drops. Ground crews came from No 168 Maintenance Unit which had done the conversion work, while the Army contribution was made by Royal Army Service Corps personnel who had recently been through a parachute course. The Flight was under the command of an RAF Flight Lieutenant who was experienced in supply drops.

But preparations were not yet complete since a landing strip had to be prepared near to the inland centres. One was quickly made ready at Qatn and, on 28 April, a Wellington was sent there to test the surface. Happily, the airstrip passed with flying colours, so operations could now be confidently pushed ahead.

On the following day, the actual carriage of grain began. Three Wellington Xs made two sorties each, delivering 216 bags in all, each weighing 168 lb. This total was improved upon on 30 April, when 228 bags were delivered.

Thereafter, day in day out, in the stifling heat, the Wellingtons continued their shuttle. The surface of the landing strip was watched carefully, since it had to stand up to a minimum of ten landings per day, but the work had been done well, and there was no need to halt the operation for repairs. A job of equal importance was that of unloading the Wellingtons as quickly as possible so that they could return to the cooler air with the minimum of delay. To this end, the RASC was finally able to organise matters so that no machine was on the ground for more than fifteen minutes.

By 18 May it was decided that enough grain had been flown into Qatn, so on that day the distribution drops began. This switch in operations reduced the number of landings per day on the Qatn strip, and most of the party who had been maintaining it and unloading the aircraft could therefore be withdrawn.

For the remainder of May the mercy flights continued, taking the bags to the remote inland areas until a total of 1,936—representing over 145 tons of grain and other food—had been parachuted to the starving people. Naturally, there was some concern over the strength of the bags delivered in this unorthodox manner, but in actual fact only five per cent were damaged. By the end of May the Wellingtons had flown 165 sorties in some 300 hours'

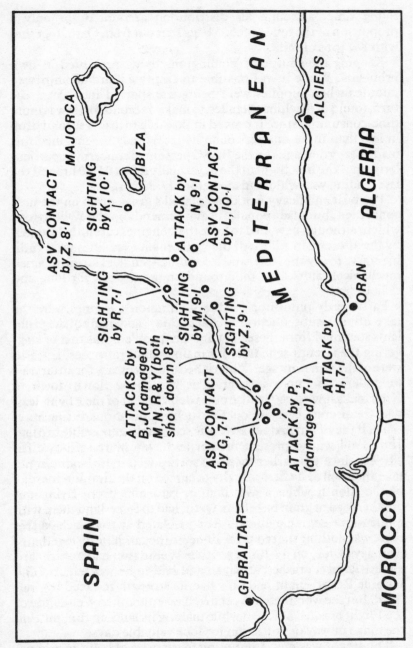

The operational area of the Wellingtons of the Famine Relief Flight in 1944.

flying time, although air distribution accounted for only a proportion of the total of 5,505 bags sent out from Qatn, together with 8¼ tons of milk.

Keeping the shuttle of Wellingtons flying presented its own problems. While it was possible to empty an aircraft in fifteen minutes when supplies were being transported into Qatn, the turn-round of machines detailed to make a second sortie was more time-consuming since it proved impossible to load a second drop in less than three-quarters of an hour. As may be imagined this made heavy demands on the RASC personnel concerned, particularly since the first flight of the day usually left at 04:30 hrs and the last landing was seldom made before 17:30 hrs.

The heat and heavy workload placed a great strain on the men concerned, but made equally heavy demands on the Wellingtons which, although new, had to have their engines carefully 'nursed' by the aircrew. In addition, the maintenance facilities were rudimentary, to say the least, and a seemingly endless string of small mechanical faults kept the ground crews at work for long and tedious hours.

Particularly punishing for the Wellington's engines were the take-offs and subsequent climbs at midday, and many of the problems stemmed from these. Yet another problem was that of staggering the aircraft schedules for maintenance purposes, since all were of the same vintage. When it became necessary for an aircraft to undergo a minor inspection it had to be flown down to Khormaksar where a small ground detachment of the Flight dealt with the aircraft, carrying out five such examinations during May.

Yet if the Flight had achieved the seemingly impossible in May, June 1944 was to present further and even more serious difficulties, since the earlier month's sorties were now beginning to take their toll. The first casualty occurred on the first Wednesday of the month when a Wellington, returning from flying out another load of grain bags from Qatn, had to force-land there with a burnt-out engine cylinder. At an isolated station such as this there was nothing that could be done, so the machine just sat there. Ten days later, on 17 June, another Wellington had a starboard engine failure, crashed at Riyan and had to be written off. The Famine Relief Flight had now had its strength reduced by one-third, but the worst setback occurred when another Wellington of the Flight crashed at Riyan while making its landing run, putting the long runway out of action for four valuable days.

The Flight was now attempting to carry on at half the original strength, and its days were clearly numbered. The remaining three aircraft had been showing signs of wear for some time. The most common symptom was excessive oil pressure, which was most probably the result of each of them having to make a climb to 6,000 feet three times a day while fully laden. Then, on the last day of June, came orders from Aden that the Famine Relief Flight was to be withdrawn from operations so that the long-suffering Wellingtons could be properly serviced. Any man connected with the eight-week operation wondered whether it had all been worth while: the answer was to come just as the Flight stood down. The Political Officer in charge of the Relief Commission announced that, in his opinion, the Hadramaut now had sufficient supplies of grain and essential foodstuffs to last for the next four months. The six Wellington Xs of this long-forgotten mission gave ample proof that, in wartime, aircraft are not always killing machines and instruments of destruction.

★ ★ ★

Another of the Wellington's more peaceable roles was that of a training aircraft, although it is true that even these, serving with Operational Training Units, took part in the first 'Thousand Bomber Raid' on Nazi Germany to make up the 'magic number'. So it was that Jack Paul participated in the spectacular end of his machine near the 'Tommy Tree' as related in Chapter 3. But it should not be imagined that the day-to-day life of instructors flying training Wellingtons was entirely dull, as the following tale from No 15 OTU will show.

Mk Ic, *L7816*, a Chester-built machine from the same batch that was to supply a DWI conversion, stood ready on the runway at the Mount Farm Satellite station with its motors ticking over, awaiting clearance for take-off. The aircraft was about to lift off for an NFT— Night Flying Test. Now the Aldis lamp in the distance winked its permission, the trainer roared down the runway and, as speed gathered, the tail rose and the machine 'unstuck' and began to gain altitude. The only other person on board was the radio operator, Flt Sgt Stoodley.

Usually on flights such as these, the form was to 'Grab one's helmet, jump in, and play around at a low altitude for about fifteen minutes!' However, any illusion that this was to be just another NFT was dispelled as the pilot attempted to begin a turn to port. There was no response from the rear of the Wellington, and to an experienced pilot like Jack this could mean only one thing—the elevator cables had parted!

They were at the standard low altitude for the test, and this looked like being the undoing of the two men, for baling out was out of the question since there was no way the machine could climb higher and, from that height, they would hit the ground before their parachutes opened. Thankfully, as trying to land the Wimpy was the only option, the loss of elevator control had occurred before the undercarriage had been raised.

With the Wellington's characteristic of lifting its nose when flaps down was selected, the situation naturally looked grave. The only answer, and that an uncertain one, was to make a landing without lowered flaps on the downwind leg and to use the elevator trimming tabs (the small surfaces in the larger ones which were merely intended to balance the controls) as a makeship substitute tail control. But the worst was yet to come: the big machine had been set on a landing approach when the bowden cables—stranded wire ropes similar to those used to operate the brakes of a bicycle—parted under the strain! The touchdown was fast, noisy and violent. The Wellington struck the ground, seemed about to bounce and then, as the undercarriage collapsed, shot across the airfield in a fury of earth, metal parts and debris until it drew to a halt and a great silence descended, broken after a few seconds by the shrilling of the bells on fire tenders and 'meat van'.

The subsequent Court of Inquiry established that the spectacular end of *L7816*, which so nearly meant the deaths of the two men on board, was due to a rigger having failed to replace a nut on one of the bolts used to secure certain sections of the elevator control rod. 'For want of a nail...'.

* * *

One of the most unusual instances of Wellington role-changing occurred when the mighty machine, at that time seldom thought of as anything but a bomber, was suddenly forced to act as a fighter, and an interceptor fighter at that.

The aircraft in question was taking off one morning when a Nazi bomber appeared without warning below the low cloud, then dropped a stick of bombs across the centre of the nearby town. Having completed his bombing run, the Luftwaffe pilot banked round, evidently to assess the result of his handiwork, then made a turn to fly over the area again, failing to see the Wellington which an eighteen-year-old pilot, Sgt Goodman, was taking up for an air test. The young Sergeant was able to approach unnoticed by the Dornier crew and flew alongside the bomber. The first indication that the men in the Do 17z were to have of the presence of the RAF machine was when the front and rear gunners of the Wellington swung their turrets through some ninety degrees and raked the Nazi with deadly fire for perhaps ten to fifteen seconds.

The Nazi pilot reacted immediately. With a swift movement of the controls he tossed his Dornier into a climbing turn and made for the cloud cover. Although the Wellington pilot gave chase, it was to no avail, and the enemy seemed to have escaped in one piece.

After landing, the Sergeant Pilot of the Wimpy—destined in later years to attain the rank of Group Captain—reported the encounter to Sqn Ldr Black, officer commanding the station's 'B' Flight. In an interview later the same day, Black told Sgt Goodman that a Dornier 17z, believed to be the one that had bombed the town earlier in the day, had crash-landed near Thetford, but had been claimed as a 'kill' by anti-aircraft gunners in the area. In the circumstances it was, of course, impossible to substantiate either claim, but the Wellington crew were placated with credit for half a victory. However, in later years, the pilot commented that he was quite certain that his own gunners deserved all the credit, adding with a touch of humour, '…knowing how bloody awful the Army gunners were in those days!' Whatever the rights of the story may be, this use of a Vickers Wellington as an interceptor fighter may well be unique!

★　★　★

Different people remember the Wellington in different situations, and no collection of Wimpy memories would be complete without reference to the type at Dispersal Units. No 21 Dispersal Unit in Northern Ireland was probably typical.

No 21 Dispersal Unit was smaller than most, and staffed by the two officers, eight other ranks and eleven technicians, civilians, etc. The headquarters at Ballywalter were suitably modest, consisting of a typical, square red-brick structure divided up inside into three small rooms which provided offices for the commanding officer, the administration officer and the guard.

No 21 was sited in Lord Iveagh's estate which covered some 300 acres of the Ards Peninsula at each side of the road between Newtownards and Portaferry on the east side of Strangford Lough. The RAF base was on the easternmost side of the dividing road with the North Channel beach of the Irish Sea forming the eastern boundary. The opposite side of the road was heavily wooded and this natural camouflage, together with some scrim netting, effectively hid the landing strip which ran almost due north to south with its dispersal sites to either side.

The strip could be used for both landing and take-off thanks largely to the fact that the land neighbouring the southern boundary and owned by a tenant-farmer rose some 18 ft above the height of the centre of the landing area. The northern end rose a little more and had its own special touch in a luxuriant growth of 30-ft high trees. These 'special features' led Wellington pilots to exercise special caution and to make pungent—and unprintable—comments. The airmen's vocabulary was even more colourful when they had to land in a cross-wind, touch down with a tail-wind or merely contend with the variable direction of the gusting shore winds.

Across the main road and near to the rising ground to the south of the strip additional interest was provided by another dispersal area where taxying offered a splendid exercise in self-control...if one was to avoid colliding with cattle, sheep, tractors, etc!

With so much natural camouflage it might seem that the single building would be difficult to pick out from the air, but this was not so since it was located well away from the trees on a gravel area near to the road crossing at the southern end. The station was in fact a satellite of RAF Langford Lodge near to Lough Neagh, County Down, from which many of the aircraft for the Dispersal Unit arrived.

Life at such a station was normally uneventful. Certainly there were no enemy attacks, and as all the personnel were posted out except for the dog-handlers, the summit of excitement in 1943 was when one of these accidently shot himself through the backside! However, the calm of No 21 DU was to be shaken one night by the administration officer. The officer in question was out on patrol accompanied by one of the German Shepherd dogs who was especially vicious. Despite Kringle's deserved reputation for ferocity, the Pilot Officer managed to handle him in a friendly manner as they made their way under cover of darkness between the parked Fairey Battle, Handley Page Herefords, Lockheed Hudsons, Douglas Bostons and Vickers Wellingtons. It was the sight of one of the latter that gave the young officer an idea: just how simple was it for a potential saboteur to merge into the background? Hardly had the question taken form in his mind than he decided to put the matter to the test, using the nearest Wellington for his experiment. With a minimum of coaxing, Kringle jumped on to the wing of the aircraft and then on to the top of the fuselage, the only sound being a rustling noise as the animal scrabbled for a foothold. Once the dog and man were safely atop the Wellington, the Pilot Officer's firm 'Down' ensured that the dog lay still alongside him.

In a few moments there came the faint sound of approaching footsteps. Soon their source became visible; two shadows cast by none other than the commanding officer and one of the dog-handlers, deep in conversation. The restraining hand that the administration officer placed on young Kringle's collar was unnecessary, for the German Shepherd lay perfectly still, except for a slight movement of his head as his nostrils caught the scent of the two men below. The pair now slowly moved out of sight, their darker outlines gradually merging into the greater blackness.

The report that the Pilot Officer made the next morning of how the Wellington's broad back could be used by saboteurs provided the second stir that the quiet satellite at Ballywalter had enjoyed that year!

★　★　★

Such recollections illustrate that memories of Wellingtons are by no means confined to the times when adrenalin was in full flow. Sometimes external factors make an event memorable, as with the incident in the earliest days of World War 2 when a pilot at Mildenhall spent one night doing circuits and landings with pilots new to the squadron: he was later told that the sound for the film 'The Lion has Wings' was being recorded that night. Then again, some memories are of discomfort or sheer endurance. For example, in winter the normally cold machine would grow colder still. Ice would build up on the propeller blades and fly off in chunks, slicing straight through the fabric at either side, just about level with the cockpit. The freezing gale that tore through the holes would mean that the pilot and co-pilot would have to be lifted bodily from their seats at the end of a trip and man-handled out of the aircraft, scarcely able to move.

Of course, keeping Wellingtons in the air was a labour-intensive task which kept a large number of men fully occupied. Perhaps the least remembered group of all is the men of the service department of Vickers Armstrong, builders of the type. The importance of their work was recognized at the end of hostilities when the Service Manager of the department received an award: he and his men had spent many years travelling round to different aerodromes, working very long hours. Their exhausting schedules were partly due to crews wanting their own damaged machine to be repaired in time for the next night's operation. This was not always possible since after, say, a bad landing the repair work could take weeks, although on many occasions 'cannibalization' saved the day, with a wing, nacelle, tailplane, etc, being taken from one machine and fitted to another. At Wellesbourne, near Stratford, the lads excelled themselves by grafting the rear fuselage of one Wimpy on to the front part of another.

At this same station, Flt Sgt L.W. Collett made his own unique contribution to keeping Wellingtons serviceable. He was chief technical officer at Wellesbourne and introduced a system that was later adopted throughout the Service. A highly skilled mechanic with good control of the men under him and proven initiative and organizational ability, Collett designed and laid out a sparking plug bay dealing also with accessories. This virtually eliminated sleeve failures in Hercules engines and the Flight Sergeant later received a commendation for his work.

Often the truly indelible memories are of isolated events such as the view which wireless operator Geoff Wollerton had from *R1454* of 'about 1,000 other aircraft' on 30 May 1942 simply because his aircraft was unable to get above 8,000 ft, despite the efforts of W/O Welch who was at the controls. 'In fact', recalls Geoff, 'we only just made it over the hedge on take-off!' Unhappily the good visibility of that day vanished two days later when a big raid on Bremen was less than successful because poor visibility frustrated both the main force and the markers. One of the more spectacular of these 'mini-memories' is that of the day when a Wellington took the trailing aerial off a Hampden bomber which it met head-on in cloud!

* * *

The most ample testimony to the Wellington's sterling qualities is surely to be found in the accounts of the variety of duties which it performed. One of its most unusual roles was that of decoy bomber— a machine sent out in the hope that it would be attacked.

The pilot on these sorties was Harold Graham Jordan, who was to be awarded a DSO for this work in 1942; small wonder, since the intention of the missions was to lure enemy night-fighters into revealing the secrets of the radar system they were using for detecting British bombers. Consequently, the special Wellington was sent out loaded not with bombs but with electronic detection instruments.

To make him even juicier bait, Jordan was ordered to fly a straight and level course as part of a raid on Frankfurt. However, it was only when the Wellington was turning for home that weak signals were picked up and the captain warned his crew to expect attack. At the same time he sent a coded signal to base saying that he had probably detected a night-fighter. In the next few minutes the Wellington was attacked eleven times and every member of the crew was wounded, including Jordan who was hit in the arm. Nevertheless, he still managed to draft a message to Britain for despatch by the wireless operator, before being blinded in one eye as the night-fighter came in again.

The Wellington was now scarcely flyable but Harold gamely set course for home and struggled as far as Deal where he had to admit defeat and make a descent into the sea. Despite his wounds, Jordan first took the precaution of flying over land and dropping one of the crew by parachute near Canterbury, carrying the vital information in case his colleagues drowned: happily, they were all rescued. Jordan and his crew had closed the final gap in British Intelligence's knowledge of Nazi night defences. In fact, his skill and expertise were still at the disposal of the RAF after the war since he decided not to return to the teaching profession but to remain in the Service, from which he retired in 1957.

★ ★ ★

Night attacks proved the most effective in the early days when the Wellington was at its peak, and the memories of these therefore remain particularly green. In those days, the enemy had a master searchlight that was seemingly radar-controlled. This would pick out a target and all the rest would focus on the unlucky aircraft while the anti-aircraft guns opened up to make an almost certain kill.

In this situation, the RAF pilots' tactic was to wait until some unlucky blighter had been picked out and then go in to drop the bombs while the defences were otherwise engaged. Over Kiel, Sgt Coleman was hoping to employ just this tactic when suddenly the aircraft became a blaze of light and within seconds was surrounded with black shell bursts.

From 15,000 ft, the pilot immediately went into a dive through the flashes and bangs to 6,000, where he levelled out and began violent evasive action. This took them out of the lights but into the range of the lighter guns below which put on 'a firework display', sending up many-coloured balls to flash past the aircraft.

A feeling of complete helplessness suddenly overwhelmed the wireless operator. Without realizing that his microphone had been accidently switched on, he began to pray, not wanting to die but knowing that 'his time had come'.

'Dear God', be begged, 'please get us out of here and I promise never to come back.' Then instead of going into a panic the man found that he felt able to cope again. 'Who was praying?' asked one of the crew as the Wellington finally escaped from the hell of bursting lights. John kept his peace, and silently switched off his microphone: there are some questions a man does not answer, even when they are asked by his friends.

All the men were very excited now, and full of bravado. They had not been the least bit frightened, or so they claimed, but the night seemed that much more clear and beautiful as John got busy with his radio and obtained a fix from which to fly home. They were now flying at about 200 ft. Suddenly there was a bang at the rear of the Wellington and the fuselage was filled with white smoke. Strangely only the one shot was fired, but it came very near to a direct hit, and on landing they found that *R1216* was peppered with small holes.

★ ★ ★

Some men seemed dogged by crashes. One such was F/O 'Chan' Chandler who collected three between April and June 1941. At the time he was flying as rear gunner in a Wellington of No 3 Photographic Reconnaissance Unit's Flight, specializing in night photography from Oakington. Once, he was returning from a sortie over Bremen with a very costly colour camera and two extra crew, bringing the total to eight, when they 'lost an engine' and the rear gunner saw the airscrew boss fall away as he peered from his turret. Immediately they threw everything overboard but to no avail, as they were forced to ditch some miles from the English coast. Scrambling out into the rubber dinghy, they found it badly torn and only capable of taking six men so that Sgt Evans the cameraman, and 'Chan' Chandler had to hang on to the side in the 'rather cool sea' and watch their aircraft gradually vanish from view under the waves.

Then came the most welcome sound of all, that of an approaching aircraft. Straining their eyes they soon spotted the source of the noise, but their hearts sank as they recognized the silhouette of a Heinkel 111. They were quiet now for a while, each wrapped in his private cocoon of fear until the silence was broken by the sound of a distinctly different aero-engine. Then, oh joyful relief, over the horizon came the welcome sight of a Spitfire...with their own CO at the controls! Within a few hours the eight had been picked up by HMT *River Spey* and were on their way to Lowestoft, warm, dry and glad to be alive.

Soon they were operating again, but a return to base in fog and heavy mist found them diverted to Abingdon; as were, seemingly, half of Bomber Command. The station was crowded, mostly with more modern aircraft whose crews indulged in a little gentle ribbing about the 'cloth bomber'. Then the fog cleared and the Wellington men were among the first away, little realizing that within the hour they would be back gain—minus the aircraft!

Although the take-off was normal, 'Chan' in the rear turret thought they had passed a bit too close to the station's married quarters, but there was no comment up front so he dismissed the question from his mind. It was to return somewhat forcibly when he next peered out, for they appeared to be only a foot or two above a flooded field. Within seconds his worst fears were confirmed by the sound of a crunch and a very long slide ending in an abrupt halt that sent quantities of dirty water surging through the fuselage. An engine had failed at take-off but the pilot had correctly carried straight on to crash in Binsey Field. The crew then had to suffer the indignity of returning to Oakington by bus and train across London, still carrying their parachutes and wearing flying boots.

Immediately afterwards F/O Chandler was sent on a Gunner Leaders' course at Warmwell, so he did not discover until his return to Oakington that night photography by No 3 PRU was finished; some said it was because they had written off two Wellingtons! Whatever the case, 'Chan' was told to report to No 115 Squadron at Marham.

On arriving there a few days later, Chandler was crewed with F/O Sharpe who was short of a rear gunner. It was on the night of 23–4 June 1941 that, returning from a raid on Cologne, they became somewhat disorientated so, with fuel getting low, they decided to follow a likely-looking coast and see where it led. When he spotted windmills on the horizon, 'Chan' prepared to spend the rest of the war in Holland, but in fact they crashed *T2963* at Debach in Suffolk. Chandler suffered injuries that put him in hospital for some time, but the second pilot was so badly hurt that he died within twenty-four hours.

Later, Chandler trained as a pilot and was offered a choice of aircraft to fly on operations. 'Chan' opted for Bostons or Havocs, but the Service, true to form, posted him immediately to a Wellington squadron!

Chapter 8
Press on regardless

The victory by Fighter Command which was to force the Nazi Luftwaffe to adopt a stragey of making night sorties against targets in Great Britain was still to come. These night bombardments would include the attack on Bristol by 120 machines and the 413 aircraft flung against London in a great fourteen-hour fire raid. Also to come was the Royal Air Force's adoption of the 'area bombing' policy initiated on Monday 16 December when 134 machines started fires on both banks of the Rhine during a mission against Mannheim. The operations involving Wellingtons were, by contrast, of smaller proportions in the earlier days, yet they, too, have their share of anecdotes.

So the force of bombers assembled for attacks on German railways on the night of 5–6 June was, by the standards of the time, a large one. Among these attackers was a force of twelve Wellingtons of No 99 Squadron, flying from Newmarket Heath, which took off in indifferent weather. Two of these were Wellington Ics *T2516* with Flt Lt Harvey in command, and *T2501*, plotted by F/O Vivian with a crew consisting of P/O H. de Forrest and J.R. Hoppe, together with Sgts Bush, Gage and Wright. Their machine was virtually new as it had completed only about a handful of previous missions and was now flying with the latest radio equipment aboard. The call sign was 'F for Freddie', and the Wimpy was marked with an insignia of crossed tennis raquets and balls.

The twelve Wellingtons flew on through the night towards Germany and their target. The latest weather reports were causing a stir back at headquarters since it looked as though the conditions were soon going to be appalling. The officers had a short conference then issued the order for the sorties to be cancelled and the Wellingtons to return to base.

Back at Newmarket, the returning bombers were counted in. Only ten came home. Obviously two crews had not received the order: somewhere over enemy territory two lone Wellingtons were pressing on into the steadily worsening weather.

Time passed. Luck was with Flt Lt Harvey and his men for they eventually returned to base, after flying around for a considerable time in the severe weather over central Europe. Less fortunate were those in Vivian's machine. Bent on finding the target, they made a determined effort to locate it, and it was only when the fuel gauges showed that the petrol supply was dangerously low that they had the good luck to come across a gap in the murk. They pounced on the window and glided through. They had no idea where they were, but were simply thankful to find open country below. After a safe landing they sighed with satisfaction...which soon turned to dismay at the sight of Nazi uniforms. The six aboard were to be prisoners-of-war for the duration, and they had made the enemy a handsome present of a fully-equipped and relatively new Wellington in airworthy condition!

* * *

The weather played an understandably large part in aircraft operations over the vast expanse of continental Europe. However, occasionally it took its toll not over enemy territory but nearer home, as happened in the opening months of 1941, when the use of Wellington bombers was at its zenith.

'R for Robert' *T2888* had taken off at 18:35 hrs on 11 February. The aircraft, with its load of six 5000-lb high-explosive bombs, was under the command of Sgt Robinson, although it had been flown frequently in the past by 'Benny' Goodman. The target was duly attacked, and the Wellington turned for base.

It was when 'R for Robert' approached the English coast that the trouble started. The weather was much worse than had been forecast; in fact, there was very thick fog. Nevertheless Trevor Thain, the bomber's navigator, brought the pilot safely back close to base. Here, however, conditions were so bad that there was no possibility of their making a safe landing so the machine was diverted to another East Anglian base where the runway was all laid out with goose-neck flares to light the arrival's path. Even here the fog was too thick for comfort and the pilot had to try to land by means of timed circuits on gyro headings. However, even under ideal conditions this method can never be relied on for one hundred per cent accuracy, and it soon became obvious that the system was not going to work, although Robinson was sorely tempted to keep trying because they were running short of fuel.

There was only one sensible option open to them now, so they took it. 'R for Robert' was put into a climb towards the north and the less thickly-populated vicinity of The Wash, where the crew could bale out and the aircraft could crash without endangering lives. That this was the wisest course became abundantly clear when, with the Wellington at no more than 2,000 ft, the engines began to splutter from lack of fuel. The order to abandon the machine was given immediately, with the two gunners going first, followed by the navigator, radio operator, and finally the two pilots.

Trevor Thain was to leave through the ventral defensive position. (By this stage of the war, few Wellingtons were fitted with a ventral turret, and the simple hatch provided a convenient exit route.) Thain clearly remembers sitting on the edge of the flap, facing towards the rear of the aircraft, and allowing himself to roll slowly forward through the opening and into the night. Great patches of fog effectively hid the ground from view, while the sky above was clear of all but a little mist.

The rush of air, as the slim navigator plunged through the opening, made him black out briefly, but pulling the rip cord was a reflex action and he regained consciousness as the canopy was deployed. The cloud below gave Thain a strange sensation of being stationary in the air and the odd idea crossed his mind that perhaps he was not falling at all. But within a few minutes the impression vanished for the mixture of fog and clouds below rushed at him and swallowed him up. To all intents and purposes, he was now blind.

Moments after his emergence from the murk, things began to happen very quickly. Almost immediately, it seemed to him, he fell through some trees and into water at the side of the dyke close to Welney. Although the willows broke his fall, they were not strong enough to support him in the water, so his first thought was to inflate his life jacket. This operation was a dismal failure and Trevor trod water furiously while he inflated the jacket by blowing through the emergency rubber tube.

Now that he was safely afloat, the navigator had time to take stock of his surroundings and discovered that close by was a very fast-flowing stream. He made towards this using the support of the willows for as long as possible, all the time attempting to work out in his mind how to cross the flow of water to the dyke beyond. The best way seemed to be to turn on his back and swim, and this he managed to do despite his bulky clothing. However, he had only just pushed out into the channel when a disquieting thought crossed his mind: 'How far am I from the sea?' This question led to another: 'If it's near at hand, in this stuff shall I be swept out into The Wash?'

In the event, his fears were unfounded, for Trevor was able to reach the dyke without difficulty. As he struggled out of the water he found himself wondering what had happened to the other members of his crew. Did he but know it, he was one of the lucky ones. The treacherous water had claimed two of his colleagues who, having survived the attentions of the enemy over the city of Bremen, were at that very moment drowning in a deep fenland drain. The navigator turned his mind to his own survival and to the immediate task of emptying his flying boots of water, as well as extracting the enormous quantity that had collected inside his combination flying suit.

Having done this, he found that he could stand up, and clambered to the top of the dyke. Here he paused and attempted to orientate himself in his wild surroundings and to decide in which direction to walk.

For no particular reason he set off to the right, calling out in the hope of attracting someone's attention. His shouts soon produced the comic-book challenge of 'Halt! Who goes there?' Turning towards the call, Trevor was overjoyed to see two men in khaki uniforms whom he took to be regular soldiers. Closer inspection revealed that they were, in fact, Home Guards carrying rifles with fixed bayonets. As the pair approached, he tried to convince them that he was a Royal Air Force officer who had baled out, but the two were still suspicious, so he was unceremoniously marched at bayonet point to the nearby road and Welney village. Here, he was taken to their Headquarters where the officer in charge was summoned.

Lieutenant Ray took a little time in arriving and, as the three waited, Trevor Thain began to strip off his sodden clothing. The sight of his identity discs as he did this seemed to reassure the two Home Guards although, at the time, the navigator's preoccupation was with getting warm in front of the blazing fire. Shortly after the Lieutenant had arrived, introduced himself and been satisfied as to the prisoner's identity, Thain was taken to the officer's home where he enjoyed a welcome meal of scrambled eggs and tea. Trevor then telephoned the squadron headquarters to tell them what had happened before gratefully accepting his host's offer of a bed for the night.

The next morning, Trevor Thain enjoyed a breakfast supplied by the Lieutenant's wife before transport arrived to take him back to the Squadron. There, one of his first actions was to enquire into the fates of the rest of 'R for Robert's' crew, and it was not long before the other three survivors joined him. All of them had fallen on to dry land, although one had slightly injured his leg in the process.

It was only at this point that Trevor learned of the two missing gunners. Knowing the direction in which the Wellington had been flying and therefore the possible location of the missing men, the four set out to discover the gunners' fate. Trevor, being the third to drop, had landed closest to the edge of the area, but the gunners had seemingly landed further out into the flood which, although not deep, was criss-crossed by dykes.

The four had not been searching for long when one of them spotted a blackened mass which on closer inspection was plainly an RAF blue battledress, soaked with water, and worn by a still form: they had come upon the body of the first of the gunners. Some distance off lay his flying kit, where the unfortunate man had dropped it, and the events of the last few minutes of his life became clear. He had landed in comparatively shallow water and had cast aside his heavy flying clothing, believing that he could walk out. However, as he waded through the water he had fallen into one of the deep drainage ditches and had drowned, as had his fellow gunner.

The aircraft, it had been assumed, had headed out to sea and fallen into the water, since the pilot had deliberately climbed away in a northerly direction before ordering the Wellington to be abandoned. From the direction in which the stick of men had landed, and also from the discovery of the wreckage of 'R for Robert' not far distant at Stags Holt, Wisbech, it was obvious that the Wimpy had not held its course. This deviation could well have been caused by the port engine failing first, so that the starboard one turned the machine inland as height was lost.

This might well have been the end of the story of the last flight of 'R for Robert', and indeed, for forty-one years, it was. But, thanks to the efforts of the regular pilot—now Grp Capt ('Benny') J.R. Goodman, DFC, AFC, RAF (Retd)—in collaboration with the Fenland Aircraft Preservation Society, in September 1982 a portion of *T2888* was salvaged, and the single airscrew blade was discovered intact. With the permission of the Jockey Club, the blade was mounted on a two-foot cube of stone close to the entrance of the Members' Enclosure at Newmarket Racecourse. It stands as a memorial to the RAF men who lived in the grandstand there or flew from the historic Rowley Mile, which at the time was the longest runway in Bomber Command.

★ ★ ★

'Brown!' The single name, bellowed in the direction of the oddly-clad Sergeant by the station Warrant Officer made everyone prick up their ears for the cry had the ring of a man who is not pleased with life. The reason for the SWO's displeasure was not difficult to discover, indeed, Tom himself cast a guilty look at his footwear. He prepared to receive the verbal assault which he knew that any NCO entering the Sergeants' Mess with white seaboat stockings for boots and a roll-neck pullover must endure. Few knew that he might never have entered the Mess at all, had it not been for the Wellington's ability to fly on a single engine, a topic that is still the subject of animated discussion wherever Wellington men meet.

Tom Brown was flying as a wireless operator-air gunner in a Wimpy returning from a routine air test over the North Sea, one cold day at the end of February. The machine in question was commanded by Bill Williams. Bill was a pilot of great experience who was to be commissioned only a little later. His valour and skill were witnessed by the fact that he had been awarded an Air Force Medal in 1938 when his Harrow aircraft had been struck by lightning and he had coaxed it over dry land so that the crew could bale out more safely. Now, he was flying the Wellington at an altitude of no more than 50 ft when the port engine seized without warning. Immediately, smoke and flame poured from the dead engine and it seemed as though all on board were destined for a wetting, if not a watery grave!

As they were only about 100 miles from land, this seemed unfair, and while the majority of the crew started to throw overboard everything that could be spared and was movable, Sgt Tom Brown began to 'belt out SOS messages on the radio'. To have a reasonable chance of being rescued they would need to give their position as well, so Tom turned to the navigator, A/C 'Tich' Male. To Brown's surprise, 'Tich', far from being in his seat, was on his knees with his face in his hands, evidently in prayer. Meanwhile, all superfluous heavy objects were still being flung out of the aircraft—including Sgt Brown's flying boots, which he had slipped off in case the Wellington went down in the sea and the weight of the boots dragged him under.

The dead engine had now been switched off and the plume of smoke from the cowling began to grow thinner. The flames had already died away, and slowly the blue-black vapour also vanished, but there seemed to be no way of re-starting the engine. Meanwhile, Flt Sgt Bill Williams in the pilot's seat was exerting all his skill to gain every foot of altitude he could from his Wellington, notwithstanding the fact that it was now flying on only one engine. Slowly but surely, Bill managed to drag the reluctant machine up from 50 ft to close on 400 ft. This was no small achievement in itself, but was all the more impressive bearing in mind that the ventral 'dustbin' turret was not completely retracted, and the gunner's footwell still protruded, adding to the drag.

So, the Wellington lumbered on for a full 90 miles until the English coast was in sight only 10 miles away. At this point the Wimpy was joined by a Westland Lysander to give moral support, but at the same time a new problem arose. It looked now as though the bomber stood no chance of passing over the headland and, since the port hydraulics were as useless as the engine, the crew tried to pump the wheels down manually, in preparation for the inevitable beaching. However, the updraught from the shore and the pilot's skill gave the Wellington sufficient lift to clear the cliffs and the attentive Lysander guided the ailing bomber to Thornaby and safe landing.

Thankful to hear the rumble of wheels over grass once more, the crew scrambled out with relief: their pilot had performed the seemingly impossible and brought them all home on only a single engine. It so happened that Tom Brown and 'Tich' Male found themselves together as they alighted. 'Well', said the radio operator, 'your prayers were answered!' 'What are you talking about?' rejoined the Aircraftman. Then, in a flash, he realized what Tom was referring to. 'I wasn't praying you bloody fool, I had toothache!' 'At least,' thought Tom as, with his boots at the bottom of the sea, he gingerly strode off in his white stockings, 'that's 'Tich's' story!'

As for the pilot, before long Bill Williams was awarded the Distinguished Flying Cross to go with his AFM, and eight weeks later these were joined by the Distinguished Service Order for an extraordinary piece of flying.

The opening scene of the brief drama had not been dissimilar to the occasion when Sergeant Goodman encountered the Dornier —as related in Chapter 7. On both occasions the Wimpy was involved in an air test, and the enemy aircraft were identical types. But here the similarity ends, for there were no RAF gunners involved in Bill Williams' case, and the first sign of belligerence was to come from the Nazi. The Dornier closed in at some 2,000 ft so that the crew could open fire at the Wellington. Calmly, Bill Williams took his machine to a slightly greater height, manoeuvring across the Dornier as he did so. Far from presenting his machine as a sitting duck, he was behaving in a deliberately threatening manner. The Nazi pilot realized this and lost height; as he did so, the Englishman followed suit. So the game went on between the two, with the Wellington being brought in relentlessly to 'sit' on the enemy. There could be only one result: the inevitable happened when the Dornier lost the last few, vital feet of altitude and crashed under the Wellington pilot's persistence. Such is war that Bill Williams himself had not long to live: before the year was out, he too, was to die in a flying accident. For those who knew and survived him, probably his best memorial was the story of his long journey home flying a Wimpy on a single engine—probably the first time that this was achieved over a considerable distance.

* * *

Engine failures were relatively easy to understand, but other mishaps were less easily explained. For example, on occasion, an aircraft seemed to suddenly develop a mind of its own and exhibited idiosyncratic, and often dangerous, personality traits. Take the case of the Wellington which had been flying at 25,000 ft in a manner which could be described as sedate. Without warning, it reared up in the manner of a huge startled horse, and the situation was made all the more terrifying by the noise from the engines which indicated that both were racing at maximum revolutions. Then, the big machine suddenly flipped over on its back so that the dirt and dust from the floor billowed up in great choking clouds: the youthful airmen inside found it difficult to breathe, let alone see.

Without giving a hint about what it was going to do next, the Wellington then dropped on to an even keel and hesitated for a moment, shivering like a thing alive in the vibration from the screaming engines. As if it had come to a decision, the Wimpy dropped its nose towards the mouth of the Humber below and screamed down towards the sea as if there was no sweating pilot at the controls fighting to halt the machine's mad, headlong rush.

Outside, the condition of the Wellington was a dreadful sight: the fabric on the geodetic panels had, in places, burst under the pressure and was now streaming back from the structure in wildly flapping rags as the bomber plunged downwards.

Then, as suddenly as it had gone out of control, the machine yielded to the coaxing of its pilot. At 7,000 ft, the engines began to run normally as the machine levelled out. 'Throttle and carburettor icing problems', was the cold, official diagnosis.

* * *

Many pilots, of course, relished collecting their personal set of 'hairy' experiences, no matter how precise and painstaking the work of the maintenance crews might be. Among the most frightening of these must surely be that of a pilot who was on an operational night sortie from Feltwell. The Wellington had taken off without problems, but it showed a definite reluctance to accelerate.

'I stooged around the airfield until everyone was airborne', remembers the pilot, 'and then came in to land, but was a bit too high when I closed the throttles.' The Wimpy sank on to the grass—there were no runways at that time—but the impact drove the undercarriage legs up through the wings, simultaneously bursting the fuel tanks in each nacelle so that more than fifty gallons of fuel were flung over the hot exhausts. As if by a miracle, the Wimpy did not catch fire and the crew escaped unharmed.

The findings of the subsequent investigation were interesting. The failure to pick up speed could be traced to the refuelling procedure. It emerged that the hinged flaps above the tanks in the top of the wing had been closed but not secured properly so that, at take-off, they had risen and acted as spoilers, restricting the maximum speed to no more than 90 mph—very little above stalling speed. However, this frightening experience was put to good use, for when the pilot later became an instructor at Harwell, he made it his business to ensure that every pilot in his care had checked that the flaps over the tank fillers were secure before take-off.

* * *

Accidents such as these at least had the advantage of taking place over home territory, but when incidents occurred over a hostile country they were, of course, all the more worrying.

Such was the case when the Pegasus on one side of a Wellington failed over Germany. As might be expected, the immediate result was a fall in oil pressure and a consequent rise in cylinder-head temperatures. Clearly, decisions had to be made, but the manner in which the pilot solved his problem was at once bold and novel. He made up his mind instantly: his gloved right hand moved forward, and he deliberately opened the throttle of the failing engine and ran it at full revolutions until, as there was little or no lubrication, it seized up and immediately burst into flames. These burned for a few minutes and were then smothered by the Graviner fire extinguisher operated from inside the fuselage. More importantly, the pilot's action achieved the desired result for the dead airscrew broke away and fell to earth. In those days there were no feathering devices and the windmilling propeller would have killed any hope of the machine reaching home over such a long distance on one engine. Fortunately, the pilot had earlier been a Flight Sergeant fitter and had been able to call on his previous training to solve the problem. A man of lesser experience might not have lived to tell the tale!

* * *

There are many stories which prove the robustness of the Wellington's geodetic structure. In fact, there is no question that the method of construction used by Barnes Wallis resulted in a machine which could take a huge quantity of punishment and not break up. It was said that the geodetic structure made it impossible to measure a Wellington, since the fuselage dimensions changed with the ambient temperature.

In common with other aircraft, the Wimpy had its individual characteristics—aside from its unique construction. Much argument centred around the question of whether it was possible so spin the type. There are those who claim that there is only one authenticated case of a Wellington being put into a safe spin, but there are also the sad tales of the men who felt that one should be able to perform such a manoeuvre and who set out to prove it. One of these attempts took place in the opening months of 1941.

The chief actor in this tragedy was Sqn Ldr Charles Van who said that he would take a Wellington up to 8,000 ft in daylight, cast it into a spin and make a normal recovery. He carried out the first part of his plan to the letter, but the machine was still spinning when it hit the ground. One of his colleagues was to comment, 'A valuable officer wasted and an almost equally valuable aircraft'.

Yet, despite such events, there is no question that the Vickers Wellington was a machine that inspired confidence in those who flew in it—a feeling that one could survive against the odds. This was amply demonstrated by the events leading up to 902524 Sgt James Thomas Ware's recommendation for a Distinguished Flying Medal. At the time of the recommendation, Ware had completed 51 sorties over enemy territory, totalling 253 hours.

On the night of 10 May 1941, Ware was flying in the lonely rear defensive turret of *T5860* which was part of a force sent to attack Hamburg. So far there had been little activity but conditions were such that the entire crew had to be on the alert: a bright moon was shining on their starboard side. They were at an altitude of 9,000 ft over the Frisian Islands when a Messerschmitt night fighter was spotted. At first it was no more than a vague silhouette, indistinct against the port side sky, but as it approached it became easily recognizable as a twin-engined Messerschmitt 110. Its pilot was obviously experienced, for he timed his inevitable attack with precision, coming in from the dark port quarter.

The enemy bore in with guns blazing and head on, to present the smallest possible target. James Ware in his rear turret watched the Messerschmitt approach with a calm that few could command under attack. Like the best gunners, Ware could tell his captain the most effective manoeuvre to shake off or make a target of attackers. The Sergeant therefore cooly swung his turret and at the same time broke silence over his intercom with three cryptic words, 'Turn to port.'

Immediately, the pilot obeyed, swinging the nose of the Wellington in the direction from which the attack came. If he was to keep his guns trained on the Wimpy, the enemy pilot had no alternative but to turn in the same direction, maintaining a range of no more than 300 yd, and doing some damage to the bomber.

The gunner's recommended manoeuvre had two purposes: to shorten the distance between his guns and the target; and to draw the night-fighter round so that it was outlined against the brighter side of the sky. Then, as the German came in again to within 100 yd, Ware took careful aim and fired with deliberate calmness; first one burst and then a second that shook the frail perspex housing, filling it with the stench of cordite.

Seeming almost to pause in its flight, the Messerschmitt staggered for a brief second and then jerked upwards, turned over and presented its belly to the Wellington. Waiting for just such a target, Sergeant Ware let fly for a third time. The dying night-fighter fell into a spin, dropped out of control, and at last vanished from the sight of the Wellington's navigator and front gunner, who were able to confirm its end.

But the troubles of Wellington *T5860* were not yet over. Returning home it was hit by fire from a Nazi convoy, although this shell did less damage than had that from the defences of Berlin on an earlier occasion, when a large splinter had hit Ware in the foot!

Other incidents, endured with equal calm and fortitude, added weight to Ware's recommendation for a DFC. He had had to bale out of his aircraft about a year earlier when it had run out of fuel, and had also been involved in a crash at ice-covered Kenley only five months before the Messerschmitt incident.

* * *

However, tales of high adventure and derring-do were the exception rather than the rule, and a more typical account of the bomber sorties flown by hundreds of Wellingtons in the war years is that of the night operation conducted by *L7804, P9243, P9275, P9281, R3203, R3217* and *R3228* one mid-July night. The seven bombers took off between 21:45 and 21:57 hrs. Over the target, a number of 250-lb bombs were dropped, together with a large quantity of incendiaries. Although several bomb-bursts were observed on the landing areas of the aerodrome attacked, as well as among some of the adjacent buildings where small fires were started, it was impossible to estimate the results accurately owing to intense searchlight activity. Indeed, these searchlights, together with flak concentrations, were bombed by a section of the same force at Oostvoorn and Texel by Wellingtons flying at between 12,000 and 7,000 ft.

True, these minor operations had none of the drama of an earlier daylight operation during the Dunkirk exodus when a low-flying sortie with 250-pounders 'blew pieces of enemy vehicles higher than the Wellington!' But on the other hand, they made a vital contribution in the war and, as such, should never be forgotten.

It was during one of these 'minor ops' that one of the earliest instances of Wellington crewmen being taken prisoner occurred. The men involved were some of those who had taken part in that night attack on the aerodromes, and their aircraft was 'O for Orange' which was on its second mission since the aerodrome attack. Approaching the target at Dortmund, 'O for Orange' was intercepted by a Messerschmitt 110 night-fighter with Unteroffizier Brandt at the controls. Although the enemy was a few moments later shot down by the gunner in another Wimpy (P/O Morian Hansen, a Dane who was later awarded the DFC), 'O for Orange' had received a mortal wound.

Sgt Jack Casseldon and the rear gunner, Sgt A. Walker, were able to escape by parachute, as were Sgt F. Heritage, the radio operator, and P/O P. Scott, co-pilot, although the last two had sustained nasty wounds. Less lucky were Sgt Selwood, the nose gunner (who had flown in *L7804* on the earlier operation) and the captain, P/O B. Power, who had both been killed when the Wimpy crashed and blew up.

Jack Casseldon was one of the first of the survivors to be picked up by the Nazis and taken to the Gestapo headquarters at Wesel for questioning, but fortunately his ordeal did not last long. News of the prisoner's whereabouts soon reached the local Luftwaffe station where the men demonstrated their contempt and hatred for the Secret Police by organising a 'raid' on the Gestapo HQ! The RAF Sergeant was duly 'rescued' and carted off to the airfield at Münster where he was treated as a guest and given a satisfying meal, despite the fact that this was the base from which the luckless Brandt had flown.

* * *

These then, were typical of the operations involving Wellingtons at the time when the type was beginning to prove its capacity for administering as well as taking punishment. It was now the backbone of the RAF's Bomber Command, and the British public was only now becoming fully aware of the much-relished ability of the country to 'hit back'. The cinema industry had made a contribution to this awareness with a classic semi-documentary called 'Target for Tonight', a War Department feature film seen by hundreds. This had centred around No 149 (OJ) Squadron's Wellington Ic 'F for Freddie', otherwise *P2517*. The role of the captain had been given not to a professional actor, but to Flt Lt P.C. 'Pick' Pickard, later a Group Captain in charge of No 161 Special Duties Squadron at Tempsford, charged with the duty of carrying secret agents. At the time of the film, Pickard was a bomber pilot engaged on such sorties as that against the aerodromes at Oostvoorne and Texel, when he was the captain of *P9275*.

This, and other wartime films helped thousands of cinemagoers to recognize the Vickers Wellington as an outstanding machine. Certainly these movies had varying degrees of authenticity and were not without an element of propaganda, but there was no point in dwelling on the less inspiring aspects of wartime aviation, such as the dauntingly crude navigation methods. Cinema audiences would not have been so optimistic if they had learned that, for example, No 99 Squadron captains had to use the lighthouse at Orfordness as a landfall marker, then the smoking chimney of Claydon cement works as a pointer to the sugar factory at Bury St Edmunds, before they could pick up the lamps of the railway signals to Newmarket that meant home!

Chapter 9
Fire in the bomb-bay!

As far as the civilian population was aware, the most active theatre of war was now the Pacific, with North Africa and the Russian Front coming close seconds. This was a false picture, for there was still a considerable quantity of blood-letting in Europe, particularly in the war in the air which Bomber Command was waging at an increasing tempo, still with the trusty Wellington to the fore.

So it was that Wednesday 21 January 1942 found the Mk Ics of No 103 Squadron based at Elsham Wolds, Lincolnshire, detailed to attack targets at Bremen. The bomb-bays were loaded with incendiaries, leaving just enough room for some 4½-in reconnaissance flares with which to light up the target. (These were the days before the introduction of the specialist Pathfinder force, but even at this stage, the techniques they would use were being developed by the ordinary bombers.)

The trip to the target was not particularly eventful, and Bremen had been found without difficulty, so that the Wellington was now running up to the target. The navigator called the pilot over the intercom in the text-book manner, 'Ready to launch flare—bomb doors open!' The pilot leaned forward, his gloved hand reached for the toggle and, as he selected the switch, the great bay under the fuselage gaped open and the pilot waited for confirmation that the flare was on its way.

'Flare launched!' came the navigator's voice over the pilot's headphones. It was now the job of the captain to ask the rear gunner to report when the flare ignited, closing the bomb doors as he did so. After one or two enquiries by the navigator, the tail gunner had still not seen a burning flare, so the former assumed that they had dropped a dud and prepared to launch a second. The same procedure was followed, with the pilot closing the doors of the bomb-bay on the navigator's announcement of 'Flare gone'.

Again there was a pause while the end gunner peered out into the night, expecting at any moment to be rewarded by the burst of blue-white light as the flare fired and drifted down under its parachute.

Although the crew would not have waited for more than ten seconds, it was at this point that the smell of burning reached the pilot's nostrils. The stench was very reminiscent of burning gunpowder. He just had time to alert the rest of the crew before the Wellington was rocked by an explosion which seemed to come not from outside, as might be expected, but from within. The bulkhead, which was merely ply blanking off the forward end of the bomb-bay, was violently blown into the cockpit letting in billows of white, acrid smoke. Behind the smoke was a dazzling white light, so intense that it lit up not only the interior of the bomber but the outside as well. Even the wings appeared to be made of incandescent silver: the Wellington had become a flying beacon. As the captain recalled, 'We quickly became the subject of intense and unwelcome attention from both searchlights and flak.'

The clouds of stinking, white vapour that now filled the cockpit made it very hard to breathe or to see the instruments. The pilot opened the sliding window to let out the vapour, but could do nothing about the light—so bright that it made seeing anything impossible. There was no question that the bomber was on fire, and that the blaze would very shortly reach either the fuel lines or the wing spar. Realizing this, it was the turn of the navigator to shout to his pilot, 'Jettison, Skip! Jettison!' The pilot needed no second bidding. He immediately leaned forward, pulled the emergency handle, and the entire load of incendiaries, some already burning, fell away together with the reconnaissance flare.

Now that the windows were open, it did not take long for the cockpit to clear. At the same time the crew became aware of the intense cold: it was uncomfortable, but more welcome than the heat of a burning aircraft! Inside, the fire continued for several minutes, but was now burning far less fiercely and the crew managed to contain and eventually to extinguish the flames. As course was set for home, the pilot soon felt free to hand over control to the second Dickie and go aft to inspect the damage. 'It was an unusual experience,' he recalls, 'to see the moonlight reflected from the North Sea, framed by the bare geodetics of the Wellington!'

It did not take long to work out the probable cause of all the excitement. That the green light had glowed showing the bomb doors open, seems certain; they would never have attempted to release the flare without that light. What had probably happened was that the navigator had announced 'Flare gone' and the bomb doors were closed again without anyone realizing that the reconnaissance flare, which was much lighter than a bomb, had stuck on the slip (this could happen with even weightier objects). At base there had been a long period of very wet and cold weather which may well have iced up the bomb slip. The flare would eventually have dropped down, but by this time, the bomb doors had been closed so that the missile was trapped inside.

Flares of this type were fired by a pyrotechnic time fuze which was actuated by a short wire link as the marker fell from its loaded position. The flare would then burn for about fourteen seconds and, at a pre-determined altitude, the magnesium candle on its parachute would be ejected from the flare body by means of an explosive charge.

The first of the flares must have lain on the closed bomb doors and, perhaps because the fuzing link was too long, had not ignited. It was the second flare, trapped like the first, that had been the cause of the smell. A burning flare generates great heat and this had melted the strong bomb beams and ignited part of the Wimpy's maximum load of fire bombs. 'The journey home was uneventful', the pilot recalls with relief.

★ ★ ★

The captain on this trip was P/O Kenneth H. Wallis, later better known as head of the modern gyrocopter organization. His skills as both a pilot and an engineer enable him to give an unbiased opinion of the Wimpy. 'I can still recall', says the Wing Commander (as he is today), 'the smell of highly inflammable doped fabric and aviation fuel as one climbed aboard before an operation, and the sight of the ''quilted'' fabric of the upper skin in the moonlight when viewed from the astrodome as every square of geodetic area contributed to the lift.

'The early versions, with a bomb load, were distinctly marginal, and fire was likely to be a feature of a crash, particularly if the 55-gallon fuel tank in each nacelle behind the engine was full.

'The structure was very flexible, and as each bomb in a stick was released one could feel the back arch a little more. Equally, on our two trips a night to the Anzio beach-head in Italy early in 1944, one could hear the creaks and feel the fuselage sag as the bombs were winched up while we sat aboard, eating our rations after the first trip.'

Little remembered now is the fact that the Wellington was not always an unalloyed success. Under the pressures of war, some corners had to be cut, and some changes were introduced which in peacetime would be regarded as premature. An instruction classified as 'Secret' and dated 26 July 1943 amply testifies to the consequences:

'Corkscrewing as an evasive manoeuvre will not be used by aircraft of this Unit pending further instructions. The only evasive action against fighter attacks that may be taken is a gentle turn into the direction of the attack of the fighter.

'Flight commanders will appreciate the reason for this, but under no circumstances should the reason be communicated either to flying instructors or pupils.'

This was a wise measure to avoid the failure of wing spars or attachments in the heavier versions fitted with the Hercules or other more powerful engines. However, the problem was certainly overcome later, since Ken Wallis recalls pulling the Wellington Mk III around in over-the-vertical evasive turns at Central Gunnery School in 1944, although on 12 August of the same year, three Wellington IIIs had to be put down in emergency landings there, following major engine disasters!

Despite such events, there is no question that the Wellington was a good aircraft and that it is remembered with affection by many men, since it was already in use before September 1939 and was still going strong at the end of World War 2. Some of the specification changes have already been outlined, but there were a lot of them and they are now largely recalled according to the duties of those involved. While pilots will recollect the 'no corkscrewing' order, fitters familiar with the poppet-valve Pegasus engine in the original versions will recall the transition to the Hercules XI and XVI sleeve-valve high-output power units. Instead of the accessory items being fitted to the back of the Hercules, they were contained in a separate gearbox with a shaft drive so that there was no need to touch them during an engine change. In addition, the early oil filter vanished and its place was taken by a high-speed centrifuge while, later in the war, a gantry was available for engine changes in the field.

All in all, even pilots like Ken Wallis—perhaps recalling the loss of *L7886* as recounted in Chapter 6—will admit, 'I would never describe the Wellington as my favourite aircraft'. Most probably have a love-hate relationship with the geodetic monster for, despite its failings, it had the supreme virtue of holding together when lesser aircraft would have disintegrated. The punishment that the structure could take is well illustrated by the tale of *R1459*, another Mk Ic from 103 Squadron.

At the controls was Ken Wallis again with, as second Dickie, another Pilot Officer, K. Winchester, who was on his first operational sortie...and what a traumatic 'blooding' it was to be!

The target for that night attack was Mannheim and, under a blanket of cumulo-nimbus, they set course for Germany. The trip had hardly begun when the first blow came: the oil coolers froze over so that Winchester was ordered to pump oil from the internal tank to the engines to replenish their supply. He pumped away enthusiastically until the pump handle broke in his hand. The young man sheepishly brought the offending lever, complete with the piston and its rod, forward for the pilot to see as proof of his predicament. Fortunately, Wallis decided that there would be enough oil in the engines to be going on with, so they flew on to Mannheim, bombing the city with incendiaries from 16,000 ft.

The return journey was marked by particularly heavy anti-aircraft fire which was uncomfortably accurate in the Liège region, but the machine seemed to have suffered no damage when Winchester took over the controls. The bomber was now over the sea, but all the men's concentration was on the cloud banks which rose in towering cliffs of forbidding grey, heavily charged with thunder. Carefully, the inexperienced Pilot Officer steered a course through these until their lowering masses left him no clear path and he was forced to fly into the murk. Almost as soon as the Wellington entered one of the forbidding thunderclouds, one of the engines gave a polite cough and then fell silent. Quickly, Wallis replaced Winchester in the hope that he would be able to breathe life into the dead engine, but nothing he tried had any effect—even the de-icing pumps, which usually did the trick. Soon the other engine started playing up.

It was dark and stormy over the North Sea when Wellington *R1459* began to lose height. To add to the troubles of the crew, the windscreen began to freeze over as they went down and, as ice sealed the pitot tube, the air-speed indicator stopped working. There was no hope of a successful ditching, so the radio operator began to send out SOS signals.

The loss of height had begun at 14,000 ft. They were now only 1,200 ft above the invisible sea. One engine, its airscrew in fine pitch, came back to life for a few seconds. There was a lot of 'throttle jiggling' and alcohol pumping which soon paid dividends for, before long, both engines were running after a fashion in the warmer air, although very badly and misfiring constantly. The sheet of ice that had formed on the windscreen also started to dissolve to reveal the very unpleasant sight of a black sea broken by huge white patches of turbulent water. They flew on at about 1,000 ft over this inhospitable ocean, heading for East Anglia.

Suddenly there were shells bursting in the sky all around. This came as no surprise to anyone—except P/O Winchester! The deadly 'welcome home' provided by the trigger-happy anti-aircraft gunners in the Harwich area forced Wallis to alter course back out to sea before turning north. Some distance out he made a turn towards the west and a new course was set for north Lincolnshire. A few minutes later, Ken Wallis detected a red 'pundit' beacon in the far distance. Reading the Morse letters, he asked the navigator to confirm that it was, as he suspected the Elsham beacon, and headed the bomber towards it, with the near perfect visibility spoilt only by the towering thunderclouds.

Within seconds the Wellington recoiled as if from a blow, accompanied by a rising note rather like a metallic twang. Ken's heart sank. They had struck the cable of a British barrage balloon, and at that very moment it was cutting through the port wing only inches from where he was sitting. The airspeed had immediately dropped to about 60 mph, but with such an experienced pilot at the controls it should just be possible to maintain some flying speed with fine pitch, the nose down and full throttle. Meanwhile, they were certainly not free of the cable which was still eating into the wing, accompanied by a hot smell and showers of sparks. Because of the Wellington's geodetic structure, the cable's progress produced a rather strange sensation. As each piece of the lattice-work was severed, the machine gave a small lurch, raising the crew's hopes that the cable had been broken, only for the relentless cutting to begin again.

'Shall we jump, Skip?' The crew, except for Winchester, was the same one that had successfully baled out the previous month and they were all fully aware of the gravity of the situation. 'No', replied the pilot curtly, for he knew that they were flying over the Humber, and to bale out offered very little chance of survival. In the event, he was proved right, but at the time everything pointed to his having made the wrong decision, for the balloon cable had cut through the throttle and control rods, and was now eating into the hydraulic and fuel pipes on the port side. As the hydraulic pipes were severed, the engine ceased to give any power, the bomb doors gaped open and the wheel dropped down to add to the drag. Yet, despite the showers of sparks that lit the whole bizarre scene, the petrol that was now pouring into the fuselage from the wing root did not ignite, although its smell now swamped that of the hot metal.

The sawing cable had almost done its worst when release came, swiftly and unexpectedly. The steel rope snapped, freeing the crippled Wellington. How long the Wimpy could stay airborne seemed to be in the lap of the gods, for the port wing had been almost cut right off. The front upper and lower main spar tubes were completely severed, so that the wing was now flapping and weak from the loss of torsional strength. Nevertheless, the Wellington was flyable at a pinch...but for how long? The only power came from the starboard engine which was running at full throttle and with the airscrew at fine pitch. Against all the odds, the Wellington reached the beacon, from which course was set for Elsham Wold.

The stricken bomber was gradually losing height. It was down to no more than 400 ft now, and sinking lower by the minute, all the time flashing distress signals from the downward identification lamp. By all the rules, this should have ensured that the airfield lights were switched on, but there was not even a glimmer from below.

There was no other choice than to return to the beacon and to set course again for the airfield, despite the condition of the port wing. This now threatened to part from the airframe completely while, all the time, the night was lit by the soaring bursts of magnesium light as the crew fired off what was left of the Very lights—the proper distress flares having long been exhausted. The machine was becoming even harder to fly now for, in addition to the port wing problem, the gyro instruments were toppling from lack of suction, and Ken Wallis at the controls was far too busy handling the lame bird to change over to another source.

They were definitely over the airfield again, but still no lights were showing below. Then, as the eyes of all the crew strained into the blackness for some welcome sight, another Very cartridge was fired and the captain thought he saw the shapes of other Wellingtons at dispersal and the Elsham runway. However, the welcome sight passed swiftly from view as he began the circuit before crash-landing the doomed machine.

The Wellington had nearly completed the circuit when it became only too clear that they were now virtually down to ground level. There were no accurate instruments left to confirm their plight, only the signs they could see through the perspex. Something vaguely white flashed past underneath—uncomfortably close—to be swiftly followed by a more recognizable object: a tree on the port side. They were near to stalling and the bomber was starting to shudder. At hopefully the correct height, Ken held off the stall for a few moments, and then the aircraft inexorably ground into the mud of a ploughed field. For an interminable few seconds the Wellington charged forward, viciously decelerating as it did so. Then it finally came to a halt with a tremendous jerk. Pilot Wallis, who was not strapped in, clung to the control column with one hand and tried to hold himself in by bracing his other arm against the coaming. But he could not stop himself being thrown forward. His face smashed into the de-icing levers with such force that they buckled and he saw the proverbial stars.

As the doomed Wellington completed its death-run, the underpart of the nose was torn out and a huge quantity of liquid mud poured in, burying P/O Winchester up to his waist. The second Dickie had been standing in front of the illuminated bomb-door indicators. Wallis had told him to smash them, as they interfered with his night vision, but Winchester had found this impossible and had therefore had to shield them with his body. Within seconds of the bomber grinding to a halt, the captain recovered and, ignoring the pains in his face, grabbed Winchester. With a mighty heave he pulled the young man clear of the engulfing mud, conscious only of one other thing—that the petrol from the split fuel tanks was pouring over the wreckage, providing the makings of a vast funeral pyre.

Equally conscious of the danger, the other members of the crew swiftly made their escape and, when they had scrambled out of the danger zone, the pilot counted them. For a moment, he thought that the blow was still affecting his vision, so he shook his head and counted again. Yes, he had been right the first time—there was one man too many in the group before him. Not only did they seem to have gained an extra crewman, but this one had a rifle! Then, calmer reason prevailed and the captain realized that the extra figure was the guard from the main gate at Elsham airfield that was only a matter of yards away!

Indeed, only the light of dawn revealed how close the men aboard the Wellington had come to death, notwithstanding the skill of the captain and the strength of the geodetic structure. The white object that had flashed past the pilot's vision under the bomber had in fact been the cliff face of a quarry, and it was into a field above this that the machine had finally crashed. There were plans to block off the field by erecting posts which were already stacked nearby, but the work had fortunately not yet been carried out! The seeming indifference of the air traffic staff to the plight of a machine in distress bore investigation too. It seems likely that the unfamiliar note of the stricken Wellington was believed to be the unsynchronized beat of a Nazi bomber and they had decided not to illuminate the airfield. Unwittingly, they saved the lives of the bomber crew, for if they had landed on a rock-hard runway it is almost certain that the Wellington would have been a flaming torch within seconds.

The final lines in the story of the end of Wellington Ic *R1459* on the night of 22 October 1941 were written by the crew in charge of the guilty barrage balloon which was flown from a barge at Immingham

in the Humber Estuary. They threw a hectic party to mark their plea-
sure in having some live victims, during which a piece of the offending cable was presented to the pilot. At the same time their dreadful
secret was revealed: although the balloons certainly prevented low-
level attacks on Hull, their 'hit ratio' was nothing to gloat over—six
enemy aircraft against forty-two Allied aeroplanes!

★ ★ ★

Although such tales show that the Wellington's durability could save
lives nearer home, the stories which remain longest in the memory
are those of events either over hostile territory or on simulated
sorties. One such was that which was experienced by P/O Mole, an
ex-miner with the nickname of 'Larry'.

The event in question occurred during a night photography practice flight. Photographs were taken with the aid of photo-flashes
which were launched in the same manner as magnesium flares, ie,
through a chute on the starboard side of the Wellington, in the waist
of the aircraft. Now, both flares and flashes were secured to the roof
of the machine by a wire lanyard, with the other end attached to a pin
in the tail of the flash. So, when the flash was pushed down the chute,
the wire automatically withdrew the pin which in turn set the fuze
burning and this, after fourteen seconds, would fire the photo-flash
with an explosion like that of a small bomb.

This launch technique had destroyed more than one Wellington
from No 21 Operational Training Unit at Moreton-in-the-Marsh
when pupil crews were engaged in flare-launching practice.
Consequently, an order was issued that, on sorties of this nature, an
instructor should always be in attendance to ensure that the missile
was correctly launched. This was because the aircraft casualties had
resulted from flares jamming in the chute after the fuze had started to
burn so that ignition had taken place in the tube, and the explosion
had blown the tail off the aircraft, destroying the bomber.

The pupil in 'Larry' Mole's care was new to the routine, so the Pilot
Officer went with the trainee into the waist of the Wellington to
oversee the procedure, taking a crash axe with him as a precaution. It
was dark inside the bomber, but not too gloomy for the pupil to see
that the lanyard was properly in position and that his intercom was
plugged into the socket. So, holding the photo-flash at the top of the
tube, he waited for the instruction to let it go.

When the word came, the pupil pushed the heavy flare down the
tube with great gusto. As he did so, his head was jerked roughly
forward until his face was a matter of inches from the top of the
chute — close enough to see that the flash had jammed and that the

fuze was burning. What had happened in the gloom was that the pupil's intercom leads had become entangled with the tail fins of the photo-flash, and the two now seemed inextricably linked.

Meanwhile, the mute witness to this tragic drama had been P/O Mole. He knew that there were only fourteen seconds to go before the tail unit was blown from the aircraft and that they were all doomed to die. Wild ideas flashed through his mind. Holding his crash axe, he even wondered if he should try quickly to sever the pupil's head from his body, thus releasing the lethal flash and saving the majority of the crew—a terrible yet eminently sensible idea.

At the same time, the hapless pupil was clawing at his intercom leads in a vain attempt to release the tethered flash. Then, happily, he succeeded. Eyes wide with terror, the trainee straightened himself and the flash fell away to explode harmlessly under the tail. It made a very funny yarn afterwards, but at the time it must have been an utterly terrifying experience...

* * *

P/O 'Larry' Mole was a wireless operator/air gunner and, as we have seen, it was one of the duties of the 'Wop/AG' to deal with flare launches. But sometimes they had more exciting duties such as that performed one night by Flt Sgt Denis Sharp over Hamm. The captain was P/O Lines who was on the last trip of his operational tour: it was the practice to limit the number of sorties that any one pilot flew over enemy territory, just as it was the custom to put new pilots in the right-hand seat for six sorties with an experienced pilot backing up, before expecting them to take command alone. Tonight, Lines' Wellington was to claim an unusual victim.

Dark though it was, there was sufficient light in the sky to make out shapes, and there, serene and cold in the sky, was an inviting, silver barrage balloon. Its very presence offered a challenge—one which Denis accepted without hesitation. Selecting one of the guns in the nearest defensive beam position, he took careful aim and pulled the trigger.

'I don't think I really expected to hit it', he admitted later, but hit it he did, fairly and squarely. The balloon exploded with a bright flash and, flapping and turning over, it slowly made its final descent, sending up a column of smoke and lighting its own way to destruction. Inside the bomber, the crew yelled victory whoops and hunting calls over the intercom to give vent to their excitement.

Naturally, a beacon of such magnitude gave all the anti-aircraft gunners within range an ideal chance to take a bead on the Wellington. As the doomed silver gas-bag flapped the last few hundred feet

Top *L4250*, built as a Mk I but converted to become the prototype Wellington Mk II (Author's collection).

Above *W5461*, an early Mk II in service with No 104 Squadron. Note the figure in the astrodome (Author's collection).

Below A fine view of the geodetic system of construction showing the wing panels (Author's collection)

Above A Wellington is prepared for a bombing raid in North Africa (from Norman Didwell).

Below A once well-known propaganda photograph of a British-based Wellington bombing up (Bruce Robertson collection).

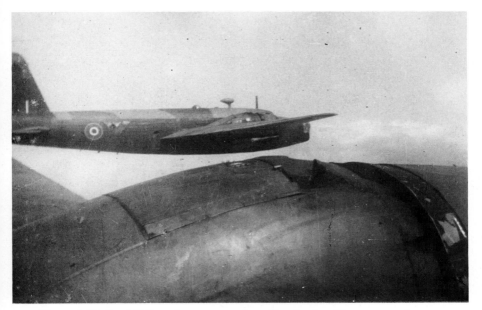

Above A Mk Ic of 40 Squadron en route from Benghazi to Misurata seen from *BB478* 'C', 16 February 1943 (R. G. Thackeray).

Below Night operations in the East meant that the Wellingtons out there retained their largely black finishes (Norman Didwell).

Above *HE115* 'N' pictured after force landing at Tobruk in 1943 with water in the fuel tanks. She had come from Malta. Left to right: Flt Sgt R. G. Thackeray, and Sergeants Art Harvey, Eric Kerbey, Bert Horton, Taffy Ball and Bob Williams (R. G. Thackeray).

Below Mk III *X3763*, *KW-E*, of No 425 Squadron, photographed in September 1942 (Author's collection).

Above left Inside *T2888*, 'R for Robert', the 'jinx aircraft' of 99 Squadron. This picture was taken by 'Benny' Goodman with a 'Box Brownie' (G/C J. R. Goodman).

Above right No 99 Squadron took its Wellington Xs to Burma for the Imphal crisis where this one crashed (from Norman Didwell).

Below *MF560* of 11 OTU, lettered *O-KJ* and seen at Digby, Lincs, in January 1945. The normal base was Westcott (RAF Museum).

Above A Wellington of No 149 Squadron in 1939. This is one of the Mk Ia types that flew from Mildenhall (Imperial War Museum).

Below A pair of Wellington Mk IIs powered by Rolls-Royce Merlin engines (Author's collection).

Above While undergoing engine inspection, this Wellington has a fascinated Africa audience (from Norman Didwell).

Below left Second pilot Eric F. Kerbey at the controls of Wellington Ic *BB478* in February 1943 (R. G. Thackeray).

Below right *HX682*, a Mk I converted to a DWI. Some had tapered rear gun positions with a hand-operated gun (Chaz Bowyer collection).

Top Mk XIII *JA416*, 'L' of 221 Squadron, seen over Malta in January 1944 with ASV Mk II radar (M. Shaw collection, supplied by Chaz Bowyer).

Above Coastal Wellingtons, such as this one of 621 Squadron (*NC829*), were responsible for 24 U-boats sunk and 24 damaged (Chaz Bowyer collection).

Below A Leigh Light Mk XII, probably of No 172 Squadron, showing the chin radome (J. Rounce collection, supplied by Chaz Bowyer).

Bottom T10 *PR547*, with yellow trainer bands, comes in to land (Bruce Robertson collection).

to the ground, the shells flew up, close, well-aimed and deadly, so that it was 'almost impossible to distinguish between the smoke from these and other balloons'.

Yet it was not always enemy anti-aircraft fire that proved deadly. The very same Sergeant had earlier escaped from what would have been a tragic and needless death. In April 1940 he had to endure a spell in hospital and it was four months before he was fit enough to return to operational duties. Back at Newmarket, grim news awaited him—he could not rejoin his old crew, for they had all perished, including the replacement 'Wop/AG', shot down not by enemy guns but by those of the British Merchant Navy. Their shooting had been rather better than their aircraft recognition, just as certain Army units could be relied upon to provide an enthusiastic 'welcome home' to British bombers—as Ken Wallis had discovered to his cost!

The first operational trip that Sharp flew with the new crew was to Hamm—a target regarded as very important at the time because of its high concentration of railways. However, a high proportion of the sorties in August 1940 were directed against the Nazi barge concentrations at Calais and Dieppe, where there was ample evidence of Nazi preparations for the invasion of the British Isles. Indeed, these targets had such high priority that it was accepted practice for Wellington crews to make two sorties a day against them. These concentrated attacks may have provided the raw material for the contemporary rumour that numbers of corpses in Nazi uniforms, charred and mutilated, had been washed up on the English south coast.

Britain lived in hourly expectation of a Nazi landing and Sgt Sharp still clearly recalls the Saturday morning when he was stopped in the town near his base by an armaments officer. Sharp was told that he had better 'report back to the aerodrome and start bombing up' as 'they're invading!'

★　★　★

Daylight raiders often received the severest mauling, but night operations were, by and large, those which were given the heaviest reception by anti-aircraft fire in the days when the Nazi Luftwaffe had not fully developed its night-fighter arm.

Progressing through anti-aircraft fire at night in a freezing cold Wellington could be 'a flight through Hell' particularly when you had to keep a straight and level course, as on a bombing run. Small towns, where the defences were often more concentrated, are remembered as being almost tougher to fly over than the larger cities. Similarly, small pilots sometimes had a tougher time than tall ones!

Sgt Brooks was, as his colleagues remember him, 'a little chap', and on one occasion, as he was not strapped in, he was flung from his pilot's seat by the gunfire from below after he had done repeated stall turns by way of evasive action. Another pilot found that the only way of pulling his machine out of a potentially fatal dive over the target was to brace his feet against the instrument panel so that he could exert more traction on the control column! Small wonder that some young Wellington crews soon began to look like gaunt, haggard old men—'nervous wrecks', as one recalls.

Then again, Wellington operations over occupied Europe could have, if not their lighter moments, at least their unconventional ones. There were missions that took the bombers across Dutch territory and, since RAF crews were aware that the people of Holland are great tea drinkers—or so it was said—they would deliver a less lethal load than the one in the bomb racks; to wit bags of tea, donated by the Dutch in the United States. These bags were tossed through the beam window and scattered by the slipstream to be gathered up later by the grateful civilians below.

★ ★ ★

Wellingtons were, as we have seen earlier, used as sea patrol aircraft, but few remember that they were also used as bombers which had an element of sea patrol built into their duties. At one stage, Wellingtons were involved in heavy bombing of naval targets, and it was during one of these attacks that the look-out, whose job was just as much to keep an eye out for fighter patrols, spotted a submarine on the surface of the North Sea. Banking round to take a closer look, the pilot noticed a seaman on the conning tower who was making vigorous use of an Aldis signal lamp. The lamp flashed away, meaningless to all on board the Wellington except, in theory, the Sergeant radio operator. 'What's he saying?' asked the other airmen. Whatever the message was it was being flashed out at a speed of some twenty words per minute and the newly qualified 'Wop/AG', with a Morse speed of, he claimed, some six words per minute, was forced to admit, 'I don't know, he's going too fast!'

Nothing daunted, the pilot took the machine round once more, but when the spot where the sub had been came into view again, the vessel had vanished, leaving only a ring of foam to show where it had crash-dived. The question remains unanswered to this day: was it friendly with a crew who were poor at aircraft recognition, or was it an enemy submarine?

Chapter 10
In other climes

Early in 1944 the Wellington Xs had been worked hard, with two trips a night carried out by each crew to pound the Axis forces on the Anzio beach-head. Allied landings had been made there and at Nettuno, south of Rome, as part of 'Operation Shingle'—a bold attempt to outflank the Nazis at Cassino. At first the enemy counter-attacks had been only partly successful, but now the position was becoming more urgent with the United States 34th Division halted short of Cassino and the Nazis driving a deep salient into the Allied line, while at the same time making all-out efforts to capture 'Flyover Bridge' and reach the sea. To counter the Nazi push and force them to withdraw from the sector, a continuous aerial and artillery bombardment had been put into operation. Now, with its weary crew aboard, another British bomber was making its final approach to the snow-covered airfield at Tortorella, a satellite of Foggia.

This was their second trip, and they had dropped their load accurately and seen the explosions of the 250-pounders. These were 'rodded' with a stick-like addition to the nose to ensure that they exploded on contact to kill the maximum number of enemy troops. Now the pilot was giving his attention to the illuminated indicator in front of him, which when 'three greens' glowed on the panel, would confirm that the main undercarriage legs and the tail wheel were locked down. However, the tail wheel light just would not come on and the skipper made the first of several attempts to lower the all-important third wheel as he circled the airfield. Still there was no 'third green', so eventually the pilot decided to give up and land as gently as possible. Before he began his landing approach, he took the precaution of ordering the rear gunner out of his turret.

By now it was already daylight and the airfield below was a huge white expanse glittering in the weak rays of the January sun. The pilot brought his machine in steadily. Suddenly, he was distracted by an additional glow from the array of instruments in front of him. He blinked and looked again. The swiftest glance was sufficient to tell him that, for some reason, the tail-wheel seemed to have a mind of its own and had decided to come down, giving the satisfying sight of 'three greens'.

The landing was gentle and uneventful. Having completed the run, the pilot turned the big machine and taxied back to the dispersal pan, thankful that he had finished flying for the night. Only a few routine matters stood between the crew and the rest they so ardently craved. With a final burst to clear the engines before shutting down, the pilot's hands went through the well-known drill which, after switching off, called for the bomb doors to be opened to relieve the hydraulic pressure.

His hand was a matter of inches from the bomb-door selector when a movement outside the Wellington caught the pilot's eye. He paused and looked intently through the perspex to see an airman running towards the Wellington and making a strange movement with his arms as he sprinted through the snow. It took no more than a few seconds for the pilot's weary brain to decode the signal: 'keep the bomb doors closed'. The pilot took his hand away from the switch.

Weary and stiff after their two trips to Anzio, the crew climbed out, thankful that their troubles had been solved by the last-minute appearance of the tail-wheel. One or two of them wondered briefly why they had not heard the familiar hiss of the released hydraulics as the bomb doors were opened. But it did not take long for them to discover the reason. There it was, for all to see. The nose of a 250-lb bomb was sticking out through the lips of the partially-closed bomb-doors with its firing rod very close to the ground! It was the type of weapon that was ready to fire as soon as the safety fork was pulled from the fuze as the bomb was released from the slip!

One glance at a Wellington shows how close the belly is to the ground so that, had the reluctant tail-wheel not locked down just before the Wellington touched down, the bomb would certainly have detonated on impact or as a result of being shaken further through the gap. There was no doubt that it was ready to blow.

Of course, the real hero of the incident was the very observant and quick-thinking airman who ran forward to warn the Wellington crew, regardless of his own safety. He could so easily have headed with equal speed in the opposite direction and the safety of a slit-trench. As it was, he saved both the Wellington and the crew's lives. It was just one of the brave deeds that went almost unnoticed in those hectic times but which should have earned a medal. When relating this story, the pilot added 'Whoever and wherever he is, I'd like to say another sincere "Thank you" to him.' Instead, as is often the way of men in battle, the airman was rewarded only by the immediate cries of thanks from the crew before they shared a laugh and began to help with the very delicate task of making the bomb safe and removing it from the Wimpy.

The very same pilot returned from Italy to England and recalls an illustration of the fine manoeuvrability of the Wellington III. This type was in use at the Central Gunnery School where it was the policy to take a number of gunnery instructors on board for training. On these occasions the bombers would engage in mock combat with various fighter aircraft, using camera guns.

These flights gave pilots an opportunity to fling the Wellington about the sky as though it were a fighter aircraft rather than a bomber. If you had a good gunnery leader in the astrodome to advise on the direction from which the attacks were coming, you could usually ensure that no hits were scored against you. Of course, these machines had the positive advantage of having no bomb load to restrict them, and it was a different kettle of fish if you were on a normal bombing mission, having to keep heading more or less in one direction, and having to contend with more than the single fighter used in CGS training exercises. Still, it was not long before the pilot was asked to 'be a little less exuberant' so that the camera guns on the fighters could register the odd shot of a Wimpy in the sights!

* * *

The theme of Wellingtons used from overseas bases certainly throws up some unexpected tales, and it comes as something of a surprise to find the name of Lieutenant-General Sir Adrian Carton de Wiart associated with them. Although he won a Victoria Cross in 1916, Sir Adrian gained his first military experience in the Boer War in the year following that in which the Wright Brothers were making their first tentative hops! Now, 37 years later, he was to go to Yugoslavia to form a British Military Mission.

The War Office had intended that he should fly from Plymouth with his ADC in a Short Sunderland flying-boat, but when this failed to materialize, he was sent to Newmarket instead to fly by Wellington bomber. There was no room for any of his staff who had to follow on in a cruiser.

The Wellington in question was not modified for its VIP role in any way: it was a completely standard aircraft, a fact that for some reason prompted Sir John Baldwin, AOC of the area, to reassure the General with the words 'I've sent ninety-four Wellingtons like this to the Middle East, and only one failed to arrive!' The General crossed his fingers and hoped fervently that his machine would not be the second.

The first stop on the journey from Newmarket was Malta. The Wellington arrived in the morning and the General spent the rest of the day visiting many parts of the heavily-scarred island before having dinner with General Dobbie, the Governor. It was fairly late at night when final orders arrived from General Wavell to fly on to Cairo. General de Wiart was aboard the Wellington and waiting for take-off when he started chatting with an RAF mechanic. The lad felt obliged, as the AOC at Newmarket had done, to encourage the Army officer. Perhaps this was because of the—to him—great age of the officer (easily over fifty-five!). Whatever the reason, the airman volunteered the information that he had personally looked over the Wellington's engines that very afternoon and could certify that they were 'in fine condition'.

Unbeknown to the General, two hours had slipped by. It had been a tiring day and he had fallen asleep, lulled by the beat of the Wellington's engines. Now, his slumbers were disturbed by urgently repeated signals which at first failed to register on his fogged brain. 'SOS...SOS...'. Then the meaning became all too clear and the General was suddenly wide awake. That his nightmare was reality was confirmed almost immediately when he received a mesage from the pilot that one engine had failed, that he still hoped to reach land but that all aboard must be prepared to bale out.

With mixed feelings, the passenger began to clip on his parachute pack, all the time eyeing the ridiculously small hole he was expected to jump through. He had only just finished his preparations when another message came from the pilot. This one was even more disturbing than the first: the other motor was beginning to lose power and they would have to ditch in the sea. As the Wellington steadily lost height the General was haunted by the picture of the RAF mechanic, reassuring him that the engines were in 'fine condition'!

The crash, when it came, was straightforward enough and put them in the sea about a mile and a half from the shore. A cold northerly wind was blowing so the crew decided to remain in the aircraft as long as possible, particularly as General de Wiart had hit his head on landing and was now unconscious. He began to recover, however, at about the time that the Wellington started to break up, and was brought fully to his senses by the cold waves that broke over the party as they huddled on the wing.

By now, the machine had drifted to within half a mile of a beach, so the party decided to make for the shore. Then they discovered that the rubber dinghy was punctured and useless so that it could not even be used to carry the crew member whose leg was broken, or the one with a fractured arm. So, those who had sustained only cuts and bruises helped their more severely injured colleagues into the water and they all struggled to the shore, only to have their worst fear confirmed by the appearance of an armed enemy policeman. Despite all their efforts, they had fallen into the hands of the Italians.

Happily, the little party was eventually able to escape, largely due to the General's ingenuity and his passion for keeping fit...but that's another story! Eventually he found himself on the staff of the British Ambassador in China, where the huge distances that had to be covered obviously called for aerial transport. General de Wiart approached Lord Mountbatten who promised to do his best to find him an aircraft, but warned that there might be a delay of several months. Realizing that he would be unable to perform his duties properly in the meantime, the General decided to go to the top and made a direct appeal to Winston Churchill in London. The result was an immediate and characteristic telegram to the RAF: 'You will provide General Carton de Wiart with a 'plane, and report to me weekly until he gets it.' Needless to say, General de Wiart did not have to wait long!

The RAF was anxious to demonstrate a British aircraft among the hundreds of United States types in use in China, and naturally chose what was considered to be a highly reliable machine—the Wellington. Now the General had nothing against Wellingtons but, after all, his last trip in one had had a rather unfortunate end! However, he realized that 'beggars could not be choosers', bowed to the inevitable, and became the slightly unwilling user of an ex-bomber Wellington as his personal transport.

To be fair, the machine at first performed flawlessly, with de Wiart making two trips in it to Ceylon—3,000 miles each way without incident. But a third trip was in store, and it was this one that was to prove the gallant old bomber's undoing. The Wellington was returning from India with its top-brass passenger and crew plus a considerable load of stores, the greater part of which took the form of 'liquid propaganda'—whisky, to you or me—loaded in the bomb-bay. The reason for this cargo was that the precious substance was unobtainable in Chungking, where the General had his headquarters. The machine was circling prior to its final approach at Chungking when the pilot sent word that he would have to make an emergency landing. This seemed 'a pity' to de Wiart in view of the precious cargo under his feet, but nevertheless he prepared himself for the inevitable.

When the landing came it was one of the more spectacular ones: the bomber screamed in across the airfield, touched down in a pall of dust and debris, skidded across the open area with ambulance and fire trucks in pursuit, and finally ended up as a scarcely recognizable pile of smashed geodetics. Only the bent airscrew blades pointing mutely skywards and the collapsed wings drooping like those of a stricken bird indicated that it had ever been an aeroplane. Yet none of the men on board was hurt and they were able to scramble out with all but their dignity intact. As for the General, dignity was the least of his worries, since he was faced with the possible destruction of the 'liquid propaganda'.

As was usual, a large crowd had gathered round the wreckage, bustling about, gaping, and discussing the finer points of the shambles that had once been a Wellington. Among the audience was a United States Air Force mechanic, and de Wiart addressed himself to this gentleman with a suggestion that he help in jacking up the shattered fuselage. At this the American's face sank and he shook his head. 'Can't be done; she's done for!' he replied in the slow tones of the mid-West, adding 'Sir!' after a pause, as he noted for the first time the rank of the man who addressed him.

'Tell you what,' said the General, playing his ace, 'if you can get her up and empty the bomb-bay, there's a bottle of whisky in it for you!' This was a handsome tip, since at that time the precious liquid was worth £130 a bottle in China. On hearing this astonishing promise, the mechanic immediately brightened up and, although he still doubted what he had heard, gave a more optimistic prognosis. Satisfied that he could do no more for the moment, the General left his ADC to superintend the salvage operations and strode off in the direction of his car. A few hours later, the worthy ADC, Captain Donald Eckford, returned to the General's office with the glad tidings that he had safely stored away the entire cargo of 'liquid propaganda'...less one bottle.

Before many days had passed, a replacement Wellington was sent for the General's use, but it did not last long for it crashed due to a burst tyre and was a total wreck, although fortunately, as before, no one was hurt in the accident. So Wellington number three was flown in, only to be destroyed on test in India. As the General commented later, 'That was the end of my Wellingtons!'

* * *

Other overseas incidents involving Wellingtons were less lighthearted, and one of these concerned a Mk Ic, *N2777*. At 16:04 hrs it had left its base at RAF Shallufa, Egypt, for a raid on Benghazi with a re-fuelling stage at Tuka satellite. The approach at Tuka had been straightforward and all seemed to augur well for 'just another mission' when the undercarriage collapsed as they touched down. One minute the aircraft was about to make a normal 'three-pointer'; the next it was skidding across the airfield. Enormous quantities of sand poured into the fuselage as the machine shot forward, smothering the nine 250-pound bombs which burst through into the fuselage with the force of the impact. 'Hurried evacuation of the entire crew', the pilot commented afterwards marking the end of an incident that not only destroyed his favourite 'Wimpy', but was also later proved to have been due to sabotage. Looking on the bright side, the airframe was quickly 'cannibalized' by the Engineering Section, for parts were so short as to be virtually priceless in such overseas locations.

Eight weeks later, the same crew with the same captain were part of a sortie directed against Tirana aerodrome in Albania. Intelligence sources suggested that no less a personage than Mussolini was likely to be there as part of the inspections connected with the campaign against Greece.

The RAF base was Menidi aerodrome, Athens, from which *T2895* took off at exactly 03:00 hrs, before setting course for the satellite at Paramythia. They had not gone far when a single enemy fighter appeared out of the night. The Wimpy gunners swung round the nose and tail turrets to meet the attack as the interceptor came in on the beam. (This angle of attack had proved particularly profitable for the enemy and led to the introduction of beam defensive positions on Wellingtons.) An exchange of fire did more damage to the Wellington than its gunners were able to inflict, but some fine evasive work from the pilot succeeded in shaking off their attacker. Although it was clear that the night-fighter had scored some telling hits, it was decided that the best plan was to fly on to the satellite airfield.

Aware that the controls were not up to par, the pilot brought the machine in with more than usual care, but he could not prevent *T2895* doing a 'ground loop' and one wing was smashed beyond repair.

In some foreign parts, such an event was little short of a catastrophe, for spares were vary hard to come by and maintenance crews were therefore forced to get hold of parts from any available source if aircraft were to keep flying. Paramythia was no exception. Isolated as it was, the landing strip had only a few maintenance staff, but what they lacked in numbers they made up for in enthusiasm, so no one was surprised when they decided to take the wing from another Wellington which had earlier come to grief. After the 'grafting' was completed, the lads congratulated each other heartily on a job well done, but there was just one sour note to dampen their joy: it was discovered that the rejuvenated *T2895* was destined ever after to fly port wing low, despite full trimming bias. But at least she was airworthy again, and in this condition she was flown back to Egypt.

* * *

It is only too easy to forget the fact that, as well as being used in various theatres of war, the Wellington also acquired something of a reputation as a long-distance machine, especially when it came to ferrying aircraft to various far-flung corners of the world. A typical trip was carried out by W/O Tom Claridge who took Wellington 'L for London', *HE118*, from Portreath to Palestine, starting out on 3 October 1942. This marathon flight took seventeen days to complete, with a hop from Gibraltar to Bathurst in the Gambia as the second leg. Waterloo in Sierra Leone was the next stop, followed by Lagos and then Maiduguri. Next Tom flew to El Obeid in the Anglo-Egyptian Sudan and from there to Khartoum, Cairo, and finally, on 20 October, to his destination at Aqir in Tel Aviv, Palestine. The total flying time for the trip was 71 hours and 20 minutes.

But, to the men of No 3 TAF Communications Squadron, such distances were routine, so that when the same crew was told to fly from Aqir to Allahabad in India, they saw this as a short hop, in particular Tom Claridge, who had earlier gained experience with No 1446 Ferry Flight.

The machine involved this time was another Wellington, and another 'L for London'—a Chester-built Mk Ic, *HD975*, that left Aqir bound for Habbanja in Iraq. The second leg of the journey would take them to Sharjah in Oman and thence to Karachi, India before reaching Allahabad after a comparatively short total flying time of twenty-four hours. Incidentally, it is interesting that *HD975* was being ferried without its nose turret, which had been removed in England because of weight restrictions.

Tom Claridge's crew consisted of W/O 'Benny' Wildsmith acting as navigator, with Flt Sgt Purcell doubling up in the manner of the day as wireless operator and air gunner. They were taking with them a 'green' crew, freshly arrived from the United Kingdom, whose competence was to be checked out on the outward journey before they returned in the Wellington, while Claridge's crew were to take charge of a Dakota at Allahabad.

They had been aloft for about one and a half hours after leaving Aqir, and the new crew were actually flying the Wellington. Everything seemed to be going well; so well, in fact, that Tom Claridge had gone aft and was behind the main spar when the starboard engine suddenly stopped. If this was a shock, he was in for an even bigger one when, on going forward to find the cause of the trouble, he saw the pilot walking towards him! When Tom reached the cockpit, who should be struggling to keep the Wellington straight and level but the navigator!

Slipping into the left-hand seat, Tom soon sorted out the confusion, fully feathering the propeller of the silent starboard engine to reduce air resistance. In the comparative calm that now reigned, it was discovered that the fuel tanks on the starboard side were completely dry, although those on the port side were at the expected level, so Tom Claridge asked his wireless operator to go aft, switch over to cross-flow and thus replenish the empty tanks. After this was done, it was a simple matter to restart the engine.

Everything seemed to be running smoothly for the next few minutes until Tom realized that the needle for one of the starboard tanks was visibly falling back, as presumably, the petrol vanished. At that very moment he was told that a stream of vapour was coming from the troublesome engine, so he immediately shut off the power on that side and feathered the propeller again. Meanwhile, the wireless operator went off to switch the fuel flow back to just the port engine, and they resigned themselves to a single-engined flight at about 5,000 ft altitude.

It would be better, it was agreed, not to try for Allahabad, but to land at Gaza instead, and a small course correction was made that took them over Nawadhi, a United States airfield. The American strip was actually in sight when, with a brief spasm of warning coughs, the port engine gave up the ghost, too!

There was very little time to do anything, but within a matter of seconds, the wireless operator had been told to order the passengers to crash stations and then to keep firing reds with his Very pistol, which he did until the supply of cartridges was exhausted. Meanwhile, 'Benny' Wildsmith, the navigator, was working the handpump like a man possessed to lower the undercarriage and at least gain some flaps as the Wellington dropped 'like a brick'. Then there was no more time for anything—except, perhaps, a quick prayer. The pilot had turned and was approaching downwind towards the very long runway that they had been allocated.

The landing, although rough, left the aircraft, crew and passengers in one piece, but used up all the brake pressure so that the machine had to be parked at the end of the runway. Those aboard were taken to Gaza while a ground crew was sent to diagnose the ills of the Wellington. On the next day, Tom Claridge was asked to go back to Nawadhi and fly the bomber in to Gaza. Thinking to restore the confidence of the fledgling Pilot Officer who had been in charge at the time of the initial engine failure, Tom suggested that the young man take the controls with one of the Gaza men, P/O Harler, as second pilot, and with this pair up front the journey was completed without incident. At Gaza, before the second crew was picked up, a final check was made of the aircraft's engines. The cause of one of the failures was highly intriguing: as suspected, a partially-fractured fuel line had knocked out the starboard one; but, as for the port side malfunction, this was caused by—of all things—a wasp's nest, which blocked the air vents to the petrol tanks!

The journey to Allahabad, which had been so dramatically interrupted, was now completed. When they arrived, Tom and his companions took charge of the Dakota '819, and flew it to Comilla in Bengal, leaving the other crew to take the Wellington back. The only memento of an incident that could have meant the deaths of all aboard the bomber is an endorsement which still proudly graces Tom Claridge's log book:

'In connection with the accident to WellingtonX LN 504 on 22nd October 1944, the pilot No. 1313813 W/O Claridge, T.H. is commended for landing the aircraft without damage when both engines had failed due to stoppage of fuel supply.
      Signed
            C.L. Stenning. AV-M
for Air Marshall Commanding H.Q. R.A.F.
Bengal-Burma.'

Memories of incidents that took place in exotic parts of the world are especially vivid. But little things, like different handling characteristics, are also still remembered. It was claimed that the Mk Ia with Frazer-Nash turrets was heavier to handle and less fast than the Mk I when cruising, and some men also hark back to the fact that, when machines fitted with a ventral ('dustbin') turret flew with the turret lowered, the mark's indicated cruising speed of 135 mph could be reduced to a sluggish 115 mph.

Other evergreen memories are of 'high workrate' with sorties coming thick and fast. An example of Bomber Command's contribution to winning the Battle of Britain is perhaps best given in one set of statistics, chosen at random. In ten days of July, the same crew made eight sorties: only one was an exercise and three had to be abandoned—two since the target could not be identified with certainty, and one when the supercharger of the port engine jammed while it was disengaged. The target choice altered during summer from industrial cities, through the 'prestige' one offered by the Nazi capital of Berlin, to invasion barges. There was also the bizarre target attacked by a force of Wellingtons on 2 September 1940: six containers of 4-lb incendiaries plus a 250-lb oil bomb rained down from each machine on the Black Forest. The aim was to start a massive conflagration that would expose the ammunition dumps said to be hidden there. This operation involved a flight over six hours, four of them in cloud, which was a long haul when compared with the two hours or so that it took to fly a bombing mission against Hitler's fleet which was poised for the invasion of Great Britain.

Later, the Merlin-engined Mk II Wellington was introduced. One contemporary comment from a pilot reads, 'They have a better performance than the Ic and will fly on one engine because we now have the ability to feather the propeller. No ventral turret.'

Detail improvements were noticed by both air and ground crews, but the features remembered vary according to the man's trade. For example, an armourer of No 466 Squadron—a unit of the Royal Australian Air Force—remembers their formation at RAF Driffield in October 1942, with special emphasis, of course, on weaponry. Driffield had been heavily bombed in the previous year and still bore many a scar, so the Squadron moved to Leconfield for the start of operations.

The bombing and 'Gardening' (a code-name for mine-laying off the Frisians) sorties which were flown from Leconfield had considerable success and very few losses. The mainstays of the Squadron were Mk IX or X Wellingtons which had their front turrets blanked off and occasionally had free-standing 0.303 Brownings mounted amidships instead.

However, this modification was soon phased out leaving the defence entirely to the FN20 four-gun turret at the tail of the fuselage which held the ammunition tanks.

Mounted on the leading edge of both wings were cable cutters—a double towards the tips, singles at either side of the engines, and one close to the fuselage. These cutters contained a shortened 12-bore type cartridge with a high-tensile steel blade set in it. These devices had to be armed before each operation and de-activated afterwards.

No 466 Squadron had its personalities, too. One of the foremost was P/O Young, who decorated the nose of his Wellington with the bearded gentleman from the Youngers' beer advertisement and added a half-pint tot with a good head of foam on it for every sortie. On completion of his tour of duty he was allowed to send a photograph of this motif to Youngers' Brewery who responded by sending

144 gallons of their best ale for a Squadron booze-up. Soon afterwards, this same pilot, who had by now risen to the rank of a Flight Lieutenant and been posted elsewhere, visited his old base. Young took time out to chat to his former colleagues while his passenger, a VIP from No 4 Group Headquarters, made a tour of inspection. That very afternoon they died in a crash somewhere near York. Only a week had passed since the Youngers' beer incident.

Another unforgettable pilot who served with 466 was F/O Samson, a New Zealander who usually flew 'V for Victor'. On operational sorties Samson always wore civilian clothes under his sheepskin coat and trousers—how he managed it was a mystery—swearing that he would never become a prisoner of war. After a number of raids, he was shot down. All the crew of 'V for Victor' survived the crash and all were taken prisoner—except for F/O Samson. What became of him, no one has ever discovered—but at least he kept his word.

There were other personalities too, whose names it is kinder to forget. One young man in the Squadron will no doubt be remembered by some for ever. He is the NCO pilot who, on his first day, was sent off to familiarize himself both with the Wellington and the countryside surrounding the base, a trip that was as uneventful as it was no doubt valuable. His second flight was no more remarkable, but the third was certainly different.

His landing approach was neither especially good nor outstandingly poor—as one would expect of a new pilot—but it was after the touch-down that the lad's problems began. For some reason the Wellington seemed to have developed an insatiable desire to mate with the side of a certain hangar and, despite the efforts of the unfortunate man at the controls, (or, some whispered, because of them), the bomber went careering across the grass and eventually used the stalwart side of the so-attractive hangar in lieu of brakes. For good measure, it demolished the flight commander's office next door. The following day, the pilot was sent off for some cross-country flying in a fresh aircraft—only to crash in the wilds of Wales.

Undeterred in their hopes of making a good and resolute flyer of the young man, his superiors sent him off on his fifth flight with the unit. They showed commendable optimism, for this time he was actually to take a Wellington on an operational sortie. While there was very probably a song in the pilot's heart as his Wellington sped down the runway, it seems likely that there was more than one prayer on the lips of his crew, for they were only too aware of his somewhat blemished record.

After a suitable interval of time, the machine returned and the pilot began his landing approach. Understandably, he had a gimlet-eyed audience, and the less sympathetic onlookers joked that they would not be surprised if the cargo of two sea-mines, each weighing 2,000-lb, were still aboard. How right they were—neither the pilot nor his crew had been able to pinpoint the target location, so they had brought the mines back to base!

Poor man, by now he was desperately anxious to impress, probably too anxious, for something made him botch the landing completely. The Wellington seemed to be wildly out of control: it came in fast and high, overshot the runway, and ploughed into soft soil. This proved too much for the undercarriage which promptly collapsed and, in a screaming, grinding ground-loop, scattering debris and spare parts as it did so, the Wellington stopped short, like a reluctant horse refusing a jump. Immediately, it burst into flames which spread rapidly from wingtip to wingtip, and from nose to tail.

The duty crew rushed to the blaze and miraculously managed to get all the occupants out safely, although the navigator sustained a broken arm. Then the machine-gun ammunition and signal cartridges exploded in the heat as the rescue party beat a hasty retreat from the inferno. Fortunately, the fire engines and the crash wagons were still on their way when the mines exploded.

The next day the rear turret, minus all of its perspex, was found some two miles away, not far from Leconfield railway station, with all four guns still in working order. At the same time, more than a mile off in the opposite direction, one of the Wellington's engines was found—this was not in working order. On the following day the unfortunate pilot was posted away...for a disciplinary course!

The machines, too, had their individual characters. One which stood out from the crowd was a Wellington rejoicing in the individual identity of 'T for Tommy'. For some reason this was always the first home from operations, but also always with a disgruntled crew anxious to voice their frustration at being incapable of coaxing their machine above 20, or 25,000 ft—too low for operational convenience. This state of affairs caused much consternation and head-scratching until it was finally decided to call in representatives from Vickers, the builders. It did not take long for these experts to diagnose the cause of the trouble: the wing dihedral was one degree out, with the result that, although 'T for Tommy' could not attain the height of which the other Wellingtons were capable, it was some 20 mph faster than the rest, and hence was always the first home!

Chapter 11
OTU

The role in which history best remembers the Wellington is, understandably, that of a bomber with first-line operational units. However, as we have seen, it had others. Any list of the many users of the Wellington must include the OTUs, or Operational Training Units, which despite their title were thrown into the fray on more than one occasion. Yet, as any wartime aviator knows, some of the worst hazards can be natural, not man-made. One that was particularly 'hairy' awaited the crew of *LP656*, a Chester-built Wellington X coded *KJ-R*. This code indicated that *LP656* was a part of No 11 OTU at RAF Westcott, near Aylesbury, which was conducting Course No 11 both there and at Oakley in 1944–45.

Jeff Brown was one of the two air gunners in the crew, and remembers the incident well. 'R for Robert' was to take part in high-level bombing practice on the local range at Otmoor, with Jeff in the rear turret. Take-off was at about 11:00 hrs, and the usual routine was followed, namely an initial climb to about 12,000 ft before setting course for Northampton. The journey there and back would allow the navigator to gain experience in calculating wind speed and direction, as the success of any mission largely depended on the correct assessment of these factors.

The Wellington in question was fitted with dual controls, and for take-off the bomb-aimer would normally occupy the co-pilot's seat prior to taking up his position in the nose of the aircraft to carry out the actual bombing. The other gunner, having no forward position to occupy, would stand under the perspex bubble of the astrodome on the top of the fuselage and act as look-out. Meanwhile, the tail gunner was more actively employed in the early stages of the flight taking drift readings by tracking a prominent feature on the ground with the aid of the gun sight, and then reading off the amount of drift to port or starboard on a red or green scale built into the base of the turret structure. This enabled the navigator to obtain quite accurate drift measurements.

Jeff had his mind fully on this task in the rear turret and was completely unaware of what was ahead. The portion of sky that lay in his view contained a few, widely spaced, heaped masses of cloud which were causing some slight bumpiness, but no more than he would expect. Then, only moments later, the Wellington flew straight into the towering bank of cumulus concealing a core of cumulo-nimbus—the herald of a thunderstorm.

As the bomber entered the cloud, their surroundings were transformed: the colour of the light outside darkened rapidly through various shades of grey until the daylight itself had almost entirely drained away. Cocooned in this sinister twilight world, the aircraft began to buck and weave violently while at the same time it was lashed by heavy bursts of rain and bombarded with hailstones.

Before he knew what was happening, Jeff Brown found himself lifted up into the air and suspended in partial weightlessness as the machine sank beneath him, then suddenly the situation was reversed and he was slammed down into his seat and held fast in the grip of the 'g' force as the aircraft, propelled by a massive current of rising air, rushed madly upwards. To prevent himself being thrown around, Jeff tried to reach for the turret structure but his arms seemed paralysed—the whole of his body became several times heavier than normal and he was literally pinned to the seat.

It had all happened so fast that Jeff was still not fully aware of what was happening, but it was as plain as a pikestaff that they were in trouble. The plane was obviously under the control of some diabolical force—being tossed about like a piece of driftwood in thundering surf. Then, within the space of a second, another change occurred. As if by magic, the matt black colouring on the interior of the gun turret turned white with hoar frost, and Jeff remembers making the futile gesture of trying to scrape some of it off with his gloved fingers.

In the rear turret of a Wellington the crash axe was normally mounted in the roof above the gunner's head. However, because he was always banging his head on it, Jeff was in the habit of taking it down and placing it beside the cocking tool which was used for pulling back the breech-block of the guns to cock or load them. Now he watched, fascinated, as both axe and cooking tool rose upwards, paused and then sank slowly down again, as if suspended on invisible strings or manoeuvred by a ghostly hand.

Meanwhile, further forward in the aircraft, the other crew members were struggling with their own problems. The second gunner, still standing in the astrodome, was hanging on to a rope handle which was suspended from the roof of the fuselage, at the same time gaping in utter disbelief as his feet rose from the floor and he began to float, weightless, in company with the empty ammunition boxes for the rear turret, the six-foot wooden entrance ladder, and all the other loose articles in the rear fuselage; all of them levitated by the unseen forces.

The navigator found himself enveloped in a cloud of maps, pencils, instruments and dust as both he and they slowly rose upwards, then back again. Many of the items ended up on the floor under his table, but there was no hope of retrieving them until the weird experience was over.

As for the wireless operator at his lonely post, he was lifted bodily from his seat, breaking the arm of his chair as he rose. Curiously, he had not a scratch or a bruise to show for it.

Fortunately, the pilot and bomb-aimer were strapped into their seats and were therefore not flung around like the others, but even so they had plenty to occupy them. Together, they were struggling with the dual controls in a desperate attempt to keep the aircraft on an even keel. They looked on in astonishment and dismay as the needle of the airspeed indicator spun madly round until the instrument broke and the pointer hung loosely downwards, swinging to and fro like a small pendulum.

Deciding that it was pointless to carry on fighting the overwhelming natural forces outside, the pilot started to try to turn the Wellington round so that they could fly back out of the cloud while there was still a chance of survival. Hardly had he begun the manoeuvre to port, however, when he lost all control of the machine in the turbulence. Ice began to build up rapidly on the wings to add to the diffculties so that, once they were into the turn, they found to their horror that they could not come out of it, although both men at the controls were holding the bomber on full aileron in the opposite direction. Preparing for the worst, the captain issued the preliminary command 'Fix parachutes and stand by!' although the prospect, that was now very real, of having to bale out into the maelstrom was unattractive to say the least.

Obeying the order, Jeff Brown actuated the rear turret doors behind him. As they crashed open, he half turned his body to reach round into the main fuselage to the spot on the port side where the parachutes were stowed. At the same moment, the aircraft started to go up again and, as he ripped off the rubber retaining cords, the pack fell to the floor and remained there as if nailed down. The 'g' force was so strong that he could not budge the 'chute, let alone lift it and clip it on to his harness. He tugged frantically at it, but it was not until they began to go down again that it became unstuck and he was able to lift it into the turret and clip it into position.

'I can barely hold her!' yelled the pilot, and at the same moment a strange feeling of complete helplessness came over Jeff. Nothing seemed to matter any longer. He felt peculiarly detached, as though none of what was happening was real and he was watching it from outside his body. He sat there looking over his shoulder down the length of the dimly-lit geodetic tube-like fuselage, and the thought crossed his mind that they would all die if they remained aboard. He began to envisage what it would be like to be catapulted down the fuselage as they hit the ground, to be smashed to pieces against the elevator operating tube which passed through the bomber a few feet from him. But he had no feeling of panic or fear, just this early calm acceptance of whatever fate had in store.

He seemed to have been sitting there for an eternity, continually buffeted by the wildly bucking machine and half expecting to hear the command to bale out. Gradually, it dawned on him that the light was growing perceptibly stronger, and then his eyes were suddenly assaulted by a great burst of light. The Wellington hd been flung out of the clouds into the bright sky and was now screaming earthwards in an uncontrolled spiral dive!

It was at this point that their luck seemed to change. Once they were clear of the freezing temperature in the clouds, the ice began to come off the wings and the pilot was able to regain control without losing too much more altitude. Never before had those green fields and hedgerows of the Northamptonshire countryside looked more wonderful.

Trapped and helpless in the cumulo-nimbus, the Wellington had descended over 7,000 ft, most of it completely out of control. This proved to the men aboard 'R for Robert' that the Wellington's geodetic method of construction did indeed make the aircraft incredibly strong. A lesser machine would have broken up in that maelstrom of air currents. When it came to battle damage, the Wellington's ability to absorb punishment that would have destroyed machines of conventional construction caused one Aircraftman to comment that he had grown used to the sight of Wellingtons returning to base in conditions that 'seemed almost to defy the theory of flight'.

A quick check among the crew of the OTU machine had revealed no damage to life or limb, although the wooden ladder now protruded ridiculously through the side of the fuselage, and some of the wildly threshing ammunition boxes had punctured the fabric covering of the machine. Despite all this, there was an atmosphere of intense relief. All the men were noticeably quiet, no doubt pondering their good fortune in having survived the ordeal.

At this stage they decided to abandon the exercise, for they knew that even when they reached Westcott their troubles would by no means be over, for landing was going to be very tricky indeed with no air speed indicator. Meanwhile, only the skill of the pilot kept the Wellington in the sky, for he had had to fall back on his experience and resort to engine power settings that he knew would provide sufficient air speed.

Once back at base, the wireless operator called up flying control and requested permission for an emergency landing but, after checking on their fuel status, control ordered 'R for Robert' to divert to RAF Wittering, near Stamford. This was an eminently sensible command as it considerably enhanced the chances of the Wellington being landed safely. Wittering was very close to RAF Collyweston, and the two strips had therefore been connected by a pierced steel planking runway across the fields to provide an emergency landing strip which was more than 3,000 yd long. It was only too clear that his machine would need an extended landing run because they would have to come in faster than usual to keep a safety margin of airspeed in hand.

Wittering was ready for their damaged visitor, for the telephone call that had announced the Wellington's intended arrival had triggered off the station's full emergency procedure. Fire appliances were manned and standing by together with rescue tenders and ambulances, and those who manned the control tower were already giving the pilot landing instructions over the radio. These were particularly precise with regard to the engine power settings that were to be used in order to maintain a safe airspeed.

Preparations of a different nature were taking place in the Wellington. The crew took up crash landing positions on the floor in the rear of the aircraft, padding themselves with seat cushions and parachute packs. The pilot made one circuit of the unfamiliar field and then, with a final check to make sure that the flaps were down and the undercarriage locked in position, he made a steady but fast approach.

The jerk as the wheels touched was more violent than usual. The big machine bounced then, a moment later, the wheels made contact again and the clattering rumble told the crew that they were on the steel planking. The run continued, fast but secure, to the limit of the strip where the brakes brought 'R for Robert' to a halt, before it was taxied back to the hangars. Here, the machine was left in the hands of the ground crew who set to work to repair the damage while the exhausted crew made for the Mess and a welcome meal. They had been airborne for under two hours—a short trip by normal standards—but to them it had seemed like a lifetime. Later in the afternoon, since the Wellington was serviceable again, they flew back to Westcott.

* * *

Occasionally, flights in OTU aircraft were enlivened by encounters with the enemy, as occurred over the North Sea at the beginning of August 1944. One moment it seemed like a routine flight, the next, bullets were streaming towards the Wimpy as a Nazi pilot in a Junkers 88 came in close to make sure of his kill.

The pilot of the Wellington, Don Saunders, can still remember the 'glowing red balls' of the tracer shooting past very close to his head, and his surprise at the speed of his own reactions. Almost without thinking, he flung the Wellington into a headlong corkscrew dive, entering the cloud below and safety. At the same time he made a mental note to remember the value of keeping an eye cocked at all times not only for an attack from the 'Hun in the sun', but also for the proximity of enveloping cloud that might make all the difference to whether you came out of the meeting alive!

Eight days later, Don Saunders was flying a totally different mission—a diversionary sortie over Paris. The purpose of the sortie was a 'Nickel' flight over the French capital, dropping the obligatory leaflets and also scattering 'Window'—the foil-backed paper strips intended to confuse the enemy radar by giving the impression of a massive force of attackers. They would take photographs of their efforts for the record.

Quite suddenly, the smoke started. At first it seemed to be only the odd wisp, bringing with it a slight smell of burning, but within a few minutes the smoke had increased in volume until the aircraft was filled with a grey, pungent, choking vapour. The pilot lost no time in ordering his men to clip on their parachute packs and prepare to jump. Already he had resigned himself to spending the remainder of the war as a prisoner.

Although the smoke grew steadily thicker, its source was still a mystery. The engines were running smoothly, so neither could be on fire. The captain called to his bomb-aimer, a brave and ebullient man, to go forward and search for the source of the smoke. The crewman turned and made for the nose, vanishing into the all-enveloping grey cloud. He was gone for a short while, then he reappeared with his report for the pilot: 'The camera is on fire!' 'Then go back and kick it out!' came his captain's reply.

The bomb-aimer vanished again to do as he was bidden and, by dint of some skilled footwork, he ejected the optical instrument into the sky over Paris. Once the camera had been jettisoned, the smoke rapidly dispersed and the Wellington crew could once again breathe clean air.

Twelve days passed before Don Saunders was able to record another event of moment in his log book. This time, he was at the controls of a Wellington which was on a cross-country flight and by now well over the North Sea. Pilot and crew had spotted the enemy fighter at almost the same time, but at first the Messerschmitt 109 kept well out of range, its pilot seemingly reluctant to attack, but in fact he was waiting for the right moment.

Inevitably, that right moment came. The Luftwaffe pilot did not hesitate: with throttle wide open he brought his fighter in for two passes over the bomber, firing as he came in and pulling away sharply at the end of each pass to avoid the avenging guns of the Wellington's defenders. It was after this second attack that the motor on the port side died, while behind it the great wheel slowly, and almost carefully, dropped from the nacelle and dangled uselessly, showing that the hydraulics on that side had been shot away. Remembering the value of the lesson he had learned the last time, Don tossed the machine into the same corkscrew dive and in a matter of seconds had found the sanctuary of the cloud bank below.

Certainly, his quick thinking on this and on the previous occasion ensured their escape from the enemy, but their troubles were by no means over. After a few minutes of straight and level flying it was obvious that he would not be able to maintain height on just one engine alone. Added to that, the other wheel was now down too, and Don remembers noticing that the tyre on that side was flat and wondering if it had been punctured in the Messerschmitt attack.

The North Sea was steadily coming up to meet them. A glance at the altimeter told Don that they were now flying at only 200 ft so, once again, he ordered his crew to fasten on their parachutes and stand by. Throughout this procedure Don had been battling with all his skill to keep as much altitude as possible. His eyes urgently scanned the horizon. In the distance he could make out a long grey shape; was it more cloud or the longed-for coastline? It was becoming clearer now, and in a few seconds, his hopes were realized. All they wanted now was a little more lift from the single engine to help them over the shore, and with any luck they might find an aerodrome. Then, as if in answer to an unspoken prayer, a large open area came into view, criss-crossed by the familiar runway pattern.

It is not the easiest thing in the world to land a bomber safely with one of its twin engines dead. However, Don Saunders was no beginner so, having warned his crew that the coming landing might not be the smoothest ever, he gently set the Wellington down, first on the port wheel and then, after holding off from the deflated starboard side as long as possible, he eventually allowed the other leg to take its share of the weight as he steered off the runway and on to the grass. Despite the fact that the bomber started to circle until the leg with the flat tyre agreed to do its part of the job, at last the Wellington came to a halt. They were home.

* * *

The Wellington was in service for a good many years, as we know, but it still comes as something of a surprise to learn that relatively young men in the RAF have had experience of the type. This is because the machines were used for instruction well into the 1950s— the T10 being the best known of the period—and trainee navigators with perhaps more than one hundred hours' experience in Ansons might graduate to the instructional Wimps for almost as long again.

These 'youngsters' recall the type as having no nose turret; 'laths and canvas' were substituted and suffered considerably in bad weather! The Wellingtons also had 'interior fittings from another age', such as mahogany doors with brass hinges and locks, although the abiding memory, even with this version, is of a cold aircraft. It was so cold in fact, that crews were in the habit of wearing anything and everything they could: under the outer flying suits of canvas would go inner, lightweight ones together with polo neck sweaters, the uniform, pyjamas, scarves, etc, while extremities would be catered for by cape leather gloves with gauntlets, silk inner ones, fleecy lined flying boots and just about anything else that was to hand! The temperature could drop so low that the trainees were never surprised to find the coffee in their thermos flasks frozen if the tops were not tightened properly. On the other hand, although he was only feet away from the pilot, the regular radio operator was comfortably warm. Navigators even used to divert a flexible 3-in pipe from the Wellington's heating system, to de-ice the astrodome before taking sights from it. However, if the pipe was inadvertently left lying on the navigation table, it was liable to melt the perspex rulers rather more efficiently than it de-frosted the astro hatch!

Just aft of the navigator's station a bulkhead divided the fuselage, and in order to go to the Elsan or to check the master compass you had to go through this door and step down on to a pair of flaps known as the 'D Hatch' because of their shape. These were not fixed down, but waved lazily up and down in flight, adding a touch of excitement if you had to cross this part of the floor at night.

Wellingtons used for this type of training were well equipped for their day with Gee, Eureka/BABS, an air position indicator, drift recorder, Mk 9 sextant, etc, so that, as the pupils progressed, low-level techniques over the North Sea could be practised at least once.

But the highlight of the Wellington course at RAF Lindholme with the No 5 Air Navigation School was a training flight in a T10 to Luqa, Malta. These flights left at about 01:30 hrs in the early spring, and the first stage—often to Istres in the South of France —took about four and a half hours, while the second half of the journey to Luqa took about the same time. The return trip, made approximately four days later, followed the same route. Many of the Air Navigation School pilots on journeys like this were SNCOs, and in 1952 there were still some Poles and Czechs among them, as the names of Flt Lt Janczur and Flt Sgts Radina and Standera at No 5 testify.

These would have been some of the last RAF Wellington pilots, for in 1952 Wimps were being phased out in favour of the Valetta. Nevertheless, the former were still in the majority, and No 5 ANS even received some fresh Wellingtons from Hullavington. This batch was particularly memorable because a message on the fuselage just under the fin, printed in 3-in high scarlet letters, read 'Accident prevention concerns you', a legend that one officer still feels was close to adding insult to injury!

The ageing Wellingtons of the 1950s were not by any means used solely as navigation trainers, for their career as instructional aircraft was far more varied. It also had its exciting moments, when a Meteor of No 12 Group Headquarters Communication Flight based at RAF Newton, near Nottingham, collided with a Hullavington school Wellington during an air test. The pilot of the Gloster machine was Flt Sgt 'Jack' Warner. The canopy had already gone and Jack was making up his mind whether to bale out or not (his machine did not have an ejector seat) when the decision was made for him. His jet rebounded from the Wimp, went into a bunt and tossed him out with his harness still fastened, ripping off all the stripes, crowns and brass eagles on his sleeves. Amazingly, apart from some bruising, Warner was unharmed. Meanwhile, the complete crew of the Wellington, instructors and pupils alike, also parachuted to safety.

Work at the Doncaster (Lindholme) Navigation School was demanding for both staff and trainees. In the early days, the staff had to work a sixteen-hour day until the evolution of a twelve-hour shift system—one week days, one week nights—with a 72-hour pass every two weeks at the end of a 'day' week. This satisfactory system was actually 'negotiated' between ground staff and 'management'!

There were two Flights, 'A' and 'B', each made up of thirteen aircraft and on opposite sides of the airfield. They were about a mile from the main hangars where major inspections and repair work were carried out in comparative comfort. No such luxury was enjoyed by those who had to make the pre-flight and after-flight checks, and cope with refuelling, oiling, topping up oxygen, etc, all in the open. These groundcrew were classified as Flight Mechanics/Engines, Flight Mechanics/Electrical, Flight Mechanics/Radio, and so on.

Checking so many different aircraft, climbing into and out of them, as well as up and down ladders, was 'a bit of a bind', so a crafty, and highly illegal, system was evolved in which one or two men, versed in the trades of the others, would carry out *all* checks. This saved a great deal of time and energy, and eventually instrument mechanics, for example, were starting engines, acting as marshals, changing plugs, driving tractors, etc. Only the radar mechanics did 'their own thing', although even they were not exempt from being told to top up the hydraulic fluid and such like!

This excellent flexible system had some surprising advantages. One was that tradesmen could gain flight experience, as pilots who were short of flying hours sometimes asked mechanics to go up with them. In this way, aircrew who needed a lie-in on 'the morning after the night before' could enjoy their rest, while the mechanic had the fun of the flight! In cases like these, the pilot would choose an instrument mechanic knowing that all he had to do was to get the machine into the air and point it in roughly the right direction, then he could have forty winks while the mechanic kept an eye on things!

These trips were occasionally a little too exciting for, if the auto-pilot was cut in, it could easily toss the Wellington into a very steep dive, since the elevator valve in this otherwise brilliant invention was somewhat suspect. Now, not all Wellington pilots were aware of this odd little quirk to begin with, and on landing they would yell for an instrument mechanic, demanding that he come up for a test flight. Sometimes the mechanic would have no option, but it was usually enough for him to say, 'I know exactly what has happened—the elevator valve has stuck.'

On at least one occasion, the 'you scratch my back' system paid off for a certain Flight Mechanic/Instruments who was chosen to go along for the ride to Malta. He was kitted out appropriately and, feeling very full of himself, he walked proudly through the freezing night air to board the Wellington; only to find that, as 'odd bod', he had to perch himself on a load of VHF radios between the wireless operator's position and the main spar! Happily, he was close to the heater pipe and settled down to doze the trip away until he could put on his 'servicing hat' again at the destination.

Despite being in the warmest part of the Wellington, young Peter was shivering as they flew over the Alps, and it was not until they landed at the French Air Force base at Istres that he was able to thaw out. Once they were back in the air, Peter managed to doze fitfully. He awoke to a different, violent world. The pilot had accidentally flown into a thundercloud which was masked by some innocent-looking masses of cottonwool!

'All we knew', he recalls, 'was that the Wellington was flipped onto its back and plummeted down from 15,000 to 2,000 feet before the pilot and the navigator, who was in the co-pilot's seat at the time, heaved with their combined strengths and pulled us out, straight, level and the right way up.' But the situation was not to have so neat an ending for Peter remembers that, suddenly, 'over she went again, this time down to 500 feet, but the two got us out once more and we staggered back to 2,000 feet', where, 'over she went once more, back down to 500 feet.' It was a case of third time lucky, for the Wellington straightened out and at last flew into a clear blue sky.

Today, aircraft are deliberately flown in a parabolic curve to achieve weightless conditions for trainee astronauts, so the reaction of the instrument mechanic dozing aft, back in the 1950s, is of some interest. 'The first that I knew about this was when I found myself in the roof of the machine with several heavy VHF radios on my back, and then floating gently with these towards the rear, before going just as gently back again, only to be brought to an abrupt halt by the bulk-head door leading to the cockpit.' He was to experience this sensation twice more! Surprisingly, the only casualty on board was the 'official' co-pilot, whose ear was cut by the Flight mechanic's boot!

The inside of the Wellington was now a shambles, while mechanically the situation was not better, as the engines were running roughly, the controls were responding poorly and it was very doubtful whether the radio would work. They were still too low when the pilot spotted land. This proved to be Sardinia and he decided to put down there: easier said than done! First he had to fly along the mountainous west coast until he found a gap. Then he had to hunt for a suitable flat field. Eventually the aircraft did land and there emerged a young Pilot Officer, five Flight Sergeants and a 19-year-old LAC instrument mechanic, all very thankful to have their feet once more on firm if stony ground.

The party was taken into the care of the Italian Air Force at Elmas, where they collected some very creditable 'present arms' when they were mistaken for senior officers, who in Italy are identified by sleeve chevrons! When the time came to leave, the seven men boarded a Lancaster which had been sent to bring them home. There was one slight problem: somebody had to prime the engines and get them started...but who? The only available groundcrewman was Peter, the 19-year-old instrument mechanic. Despite his tender years, Peter carried out the duty with aplomb—thanks to the 'all hands to the pumps' training of the Wimpy groundcrew at Lindholme!

Back home in England, winter gave way to early spring, and a new intake of very green acting Pilot Officers arrived to train on the Wellington T10s. When these lads were let loose on the airfield, they behaved as if they had never seen an aeroplane at close quarters before. But the ground crews were ready for them. It was a rare 'new boy' who could resist climbing up the ladder and peering inside with his head and shoulders just inside the hatch. As it happened, the exhaust vent for the air-operated brakes was sited just under the pilot's seat. The moment when a curious trainee peeked in was taken as a signal for the Flight mechanics to let off the air brakes—what happened next is best left to the imagination!

Without question, some of the Wellingtons were becoming, in the words of one Corporal, 'decrepit', by this time. At least one Wellington T10, flying from a station with a poor servicing record, crashed into a hangar on take-off in fog, with the loss of the entire crew, as well as the aircraft. But even though the Wellingtons were nearing the end of their service life, they had to be kept flying, and sometimes appearances were deceptive.

On one occasion, a groundcrew had been assembled and, with no word of explanation, had been told to take their hand tools and pile into a Wimpy which would take them to the grass airfield at Sywell, Northants. There in the corner stood an elderly Wellington and the men were told to give it just a pre-flight check. Even the most superficial examination revealed that it was in a bad way: the tyres were flat—as were the batteries—it needed both petrol and oil, and there was no compass card.

However, these tradesmen knew their job and, amid clouds of blue smoke, the motors were finally coaxed into life. 'It's OK,' their 'Chiefy' was told a little later, '...after a style!' With that they all traipsed off towards the Wellington that had brought them. They were about to board when they were stopped in their tracks by a cry from their supervisor of 'Oh no you don't!' They paused and faced the speaker with looks of bewilderment. 'You lot', he barked, 'are going back in *that* one!' pointing to the moth-eaten specimen they had just worked on. With muttered remarks about sadism and ingratitude, they had no choice but to retrace their steps to the pitiful T10. It not only flew, but flew well!

★ ★ ★

Many humorous anecdotes remain from wartime, but even instructional courses have their hilarious moments. One of the classics from the Wellington's terminal days was the time when trainee navigators, taught to a fine pitch of efficiency to use the Mk 14 bombsight, had their big chance to drop real missiles in the form of 25-pounder smoke bombs on the bombing range at Theddlethorpe in Lincolnshire. It was to be one of those days when *everything* goes wrong.

The first bombs away scored direct hits...sad to say these were on the marker arrows pointing the way to the range, but a long way from it. The next stick was nearer the intended target, but not near enough, for it straddled the hut where personnel kept a score of the hits. It is a great pity that the entries in the log for this particular salvo are lost to posterity! Similarly, there is no record of the scorers' reactions, which would have made interesting reading. Particularly so, since, as soon as the observers had had time to regain their composure after the earlier incident, and were watching the Wellington vanish into the distance, they would have realized that the bomb-aimer had operated the jettison switch, for everything. . . but everything. . . fell on to the range—bomb carriers, bomb racks, the lot!

The bizarre incidents of that day were not restricted to that unhappy bomber crew and the men on the range. Fate had one more trick up her sleeve, and this was reserved for the delectation of those on the airfield. The Wellingtons had returned safely from Theddlethorpe and had taxied in. In the time-honoured manner the ground staff were signalling 'Clear bomb doors' to the pilots, who would then open them to release the hydraulic pressure. Inevitably, on that day of days, there had to be one machine which, as the doors opened, deposited some 25-pounders on the ground with a dull and ominous thud!

★ ★ ★

However, amusing tales from the last days of the Wellington bomber are by no means confined to the aircrews, as witness a memory of a new batch of fitters and riggers who had come from St Athan. They knew 'all about the Wimpy', so four of them were detailed to refuelling duty after a T10 had landed. The procedure was simple: first you unbuttoned a couple of fasteners in the wings where the petrol tanks were located, and then you lifted up a hinged flap. You could then see, a few inches down, the fuel tank with its filler cap, locked with a length of iron wire. You simply cut the wire, unscrewed the cap, then filled her up. Nothing to it!

Obviously, the luckless quartet had never refuelled a T10 in their lives, since they asked where to put the petrol in. When they were directed to the wings, they opened up a couple of access flaps, stuck in the refuelling nozzles and filled up each wing with hundreds of gallons of high-octane aviation spirit…it poured out of every conceivable orifice: the ailerons, the flaps, into the fuselage, and even the navigation lights! That aircraft had to be towed to a remote spot and allowed to dry out for several days!

★ ★ ★

As the summer drifted into the autumn of 1952, so the Wellingtons slowly disappeared from the skies. Perhaps their last public appearance in any numbers was on that year's Battle of Britain day. Although the Wimpy's flying days were over, it lingered on in ground instruction. Ron Smith recalls Wellingtons at Henlow being used for practice engine starts. The Aircraftmen waiting their turn in the rear would happily occupy their time by swinging the turret and by triggering the emergency release to open the doors suddenly and deposit some surprised colleague on the hangar floor outside!

Now, of the more than 11,000 Wellingtons that were built, only a single complete specimen survives; but the memories live on. The frightening view *through* a geodetic wing is etched in the memory of one man to this day: somewhere over the Isle of Man, in 1941, he learned that Wimpy patches were not just doped on to the fabric, but sewn on, too! That faithful old aircraft may be gone, but she's certainly not forgotten!

Appendix 1

Representative operations by Wellingtons of No 149 Squadron in the summer of 1940, including those carried out by *P9248* or *T2458* commanded, unless otherwise stated, by Sgt Harrison.

Date	Operation/Target	Time airborne
July 9	Aircraft recalled at coast.	1 hr.
11	Bremen-Schipol, but bombs brought back due to cloud.	7 hrs 15 mins, 4 hrs 30 mins in cloud.
13	Oil refinery at Duisburg.	5 hrs 10 mins, 2 hrs in cloud.
21	Bremen docks.	6 hrs 15 mins.
23	Gotha.	6 hrs 40 mins, 2 hrs 30 mins in cloud.
25	The Ruhr.	4 hrs 30 mins, 4 hrs in cloud.
28	Fighter affiliation exercise at Kirton-in-Lindsay with *Defiants* of 264 Squadron.	1 hr 35 mins.
29	One Wellington turned back with supercharger jammed in disengaged position.	2 hrs 15 mins, 2 hrs in cloud.
Aug 1	Oil refinery at Duisberg.	4 hrs 20 mins, 3 hrs 50 mins in cloud.
13	Frankfurt. No bombs dropped due to haze.	5 hrs 50 mins, 5 hrs 15 mins in cloud.
16	Kolleda aircraft park, plus low-level shoot-up.	7 hrs 15 mins, 1 hr in cloud.
23	Mannheim.	5 hrs 30 mins, 4 hrs in cloud.
25	Berlin. First raid on German capital, little anti-aircraft fire.	7 hrs 5 mins, 6 hrs in cloud.

27	Battle-cruiser *Gneisenau* at Kiel.	5 hrs 50 mins, 4 hrs 20 mins in cloud.
30	Berlin. Bombs dropped from 3,000 ft due to cloud base down to 5,000. Heavy anti-aircraft fire.	7 hrs 20 mins, 6 hrs in cloud.
Sept 2	Black Forest.	6 hrs 30 mins, 4 hrs in cloud.
15	Calais, concentration of invasion barges.	2 hrs 15 mins (P/O Davis in command.
21	Invasion barges at Dunkirk.	

End of crew's tour of duty after 30 operations.

Appendix 2

The quantity and type of flying, which made its demands on both men and machines, cannot be gauged from recollections alone. The best way of appreciating this is by looking at a statistical analysis. It seems a pity that history should be denied information of this type, so in order that the stories in this volume may be set in their true context, this break-down of the operations carried out by a single pilot, Flt Sgt R.G. Thackeray of 40 Squadron, is appended.

Use of Individual Wellingtons

Serial number	Individual Identity	Trips
R1182	D	3
BB478	C	2
BB516	A	3
DV566	P	3
HE107	C	2
HE108	L	11
HE115	N	8
HF904	D	1
HX382	M	4
HX389	J	1
HX392	K	1
HX673	O	1

Bombing Operations on a Monthly basis

Month and year	Number of trips
October 1942	8
November 1942	9
December 1942	13
January 1943	7
February 1943	3
TOTAL OPERATIONS	40

Operations from Individual Bases

	Number of trips
Kabret	10
ALG104	2
ALG22A	2
Misurata	2
Malta	23
TOTAL OPERATIONS	40

Targets

Tunis	6
Battle area near Alamein	7
Tripoli	3
Trapani	3
Palermo	3
Sousse	3
Comiso	2
Bizerta	2
Tobruk	5
Crete	1
Sfax	1
Catania	1
Gabes	1
To and from Malta	2
TOTAL OPERATIONS	40

Bomb Loads

Maximum (to Gabes)	4,500 lb
Minimum (to Kastelli Pediada on Crete)	1,500 lb
Average	2,935 lb
Tonnage of bombs dropped	52.333 tons
Tonnage of bombs brought back due to cloud	6
Number of trips flown as second pilot	12
Number of trips flown as captain	28
TOTAL OPERATIONS	40

Ferry Flights November 1942–February 1943

Date	Destination	
26 November 1942	Malta	
22 January 1943	Kabret	
8 February 1943	Benghazi }	Continuation flight
16 February 1943	Misurata }	

Appendix 3

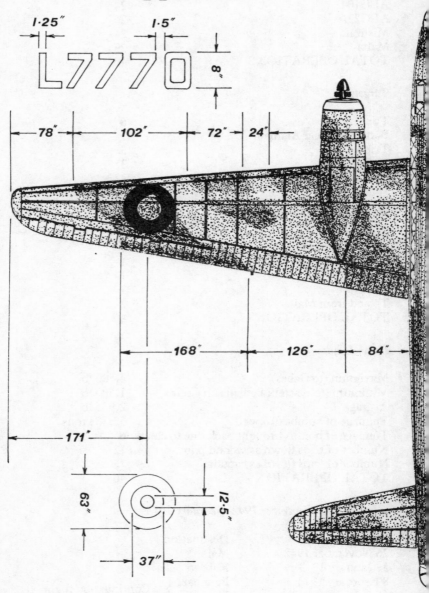

The official bomber camouflage scheme showing also (top left) fuselage serial, (lower left) underwing roundel, (top right) later DTD mark, (lower right) sixty-degree tangent division between upper and lower colours, and earlier DTD number style.

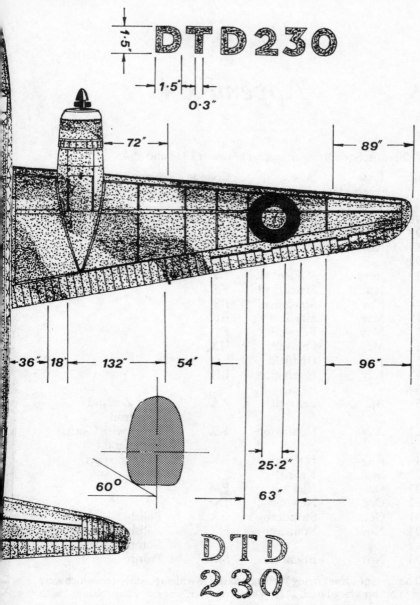

Appendix 4

Wellington Squadrons equipped between 1938 and 1945

Sqn	First received	Base	Code at the time*	Notes
1938				
99	Oct	Mildenhall	VF	
38	Nov	Marham	NH	
1939				
149	Jan	Mildenhall	LY	
9	Jan	Stradishall	KA	
148	Mar	Stradishall	BS	
115	Mar	Marham	BK	
37	May	Feltwell	FJ	
214	May	Feltwell	UX	
75	June	Driffield	FO	
215	July	Honington	BH	
1940				
75	Apr	Feltwell	AA	New Zealand squadron
311	Aug	Honington	KX	Czech with Coastal Command
24	Aug	Hendon	ZK	VIP transport
70	Sept	Kabrit		Egypt
103	Oct	Newton	PM	
150	Oct	Newton	JN	
301	Oct	Swinderby	GR	Polish
304	Nov	Bramcote	NZ	Polish with Coastal Command
305	Nov	Bramcote	SM	Polish

* The first squadrons flying Wellingtons did so without code letters which were not to be introduced until 1938. These were, without exception, changed with the outbreak of war in September 1939.

40	Nov	Wyton	BL	
218	Nov	Marham	HA	
57	Nov	Feltwell	DX	
15	Nov	Wyton	LS	
142	Nov	Binbrook	QT	
12	Nov	Binbrook	PH	
221	Nov	Bircham Newton		With Coastal Command
93	Dec	Middle Wallop	HN	One Flight
109	Dec	Boscombe Down	HS	
300	Dec	Swinderby	BH	Polish
1941				
104	Mar	Driffield	EP	
101	Apr	West Raynham	SR	
405	May	Driffield	LQ	Canadian
108	Aug	Kabrit	LG	Egypt
458	Aug	Holme-on-Spalding Moor		Leigh Light, Australian
460	Nov	Molesworth	UV	Australian
1942				
419	Jan	Mildenhall	VR	Canadian
162	Jan	Shallufa		Special duties
156	Feb	Alconbury	GT	
158	Feb	Driffield	NP	
215	Mar	Newmarket	LG	
172	Apr	Chivenor	WN	Leigh Light, Canadian with Coastal Command
425	July	Dishforth	KW	Canadian
420	Aug	Skipton	PT	Canadian
69	Aug	Luqa	WM	
179	Sept	Wick	OZ	Leigh Light
466	Oct	Driffield	HD	Australian
544	Oct	Benson		With Coastal Command and PRU
547	Oct	Holmsley South		With Coastal Command
424	Oct	Topcliffe	QB	Canadian
426	Oct	Dishforth	OW	Canadian
199	Nov	Blyton	EX	
427	Nov	Croft	ZL	Canadian

429	Nov	East Moor	AL	Canadian
428	Nov	Dalton	NA	Canadian
196	Dec	Driffield	ZO	
612	Dec	Wick	WL	With Coastal Command
431	Dec	Burn	SE	Canadian
36	Dec	Tanjore	RW	India with Coastal Command

1943

192	Jan	Gransden Lodge	DT	
166	Jan	Kirmington	AS	
407	Jan	Docking		Canadian with Coastal
432	May	Skipton-on-Swale	QO	Canadian
415	Sept	Thorney	NH	Canadian with Coastal
621	Sept	Port Reitz		GR
203	Oct	Landing Ground 91	CJ	
344	Nov	Dakar		Free-French
8	Dec	Aden		Special duties

1942

244	Feb	Masirah		
524	Apr	Davidstow Moor		With Coastal Command
14	Oct	Chivenor	CX	Leigh Light with Coastal Command
232	Nov	Stoney Cross		Transport
242	Nov	Stoney Cross	KY	Canadian

1945

527	May	Digby	WN	Radar calibration
281	Sept	Ballykelly	FA	Air-sea rescue

Index